AF207306

Simon Tatomir

Deal Selection and Investor Value-Added in Entrepreneurial Equity Financing

New Evidence from Venture Capital and Crowdfunding

 Nomos

The Deutsche Nationalbibliothek lists this publication in the
Deutsche Nationalbibliografie; detailed bibliographic data
are available on the Internet at http://dnb.d-nb.de

a.t.: Darmstadt, Technische Universität Darmstadt, Dissertation, 2019

ISBN   978-3-8487-6632-1 (Print)
         978-3-7489-0712-1 (ePDF)

British Library Cataloguing-in-Publication Data
A catalogue record for this book is available from the British Library.

ISBN   978-3-8487-6632-1 (Print)
         978-3-7489-0712-1 (ePDF)

Library of Congress Cataloging-in-Publication Data
Tatomir, Simon
Deal Selection and Investor Value-Added in Entrepreneurial Equity Financing
New Evidence from Venture Capital and Crowdfunding
Simon Tatomir
175 pp.
Includes bibliographic references.

ISBN   978-3-8487-6632-1 (Print)
         978-3-7489-0712-1 (ePDF)

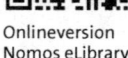

Onlineversion
Nomos eLibrary

D 17

1st Edition 2020
© Nomos Verlagsgesellschaft, Baden-Baden, Germany 2020. Printed and bound in
Germany.

Table of Contents

List of Tables

List of Figures

List of Abbreviations

BA   Business angel
BVC   Bank-affiliated venture capital
CLR   Conditional likelihood ratio
CUE   Continuously updated GMM estimator
CVC   Corporate venture capital
ECF   Equity-crowdfunded
FE   Fixed effects
FULL   Fuller's limited information maximum likelihood
GDP   Gross domestic product
GMM   Generalised method of moments
GVC   Governmental venture capital
HHI   Herfindahl-Hirschman-Index
ICA   Index of competitive advantage
IPO   Initial public offering
IRR   Internal rates of return
IT   Information technology
IV   Instrumental variables
IVC   Independent venture capital
JOBS   Jumpstart Our Business Startups Act
LIML   Limited information maximum likelihood
OLS   Ordinary least squares
p   p-value
RQ   Research question
SD   Standard deviation
SE   Standard error
SIC   Standard industry classification codes
US   United States of America
USD   United States Dollar
VC   Venture capital
VIF   Variance inflation factor
w/   With
w/o   Without

1 Introduction and Motivation

1.1 Research Topic and Motivation

The impact of entrepreneurial ventures on the lives of people around the globe is profound. To illustrate this, consider that, during the time that this text was being written, hundreds of millions of people stayed in touch with their friends using WhatsApp, posted photos on Instagram, listened to music on Spotify, ordered a ride with Uber or stayed in an AirBnB flat. None of these billion-dollar-companies existed around 10 years ago. However, every single one of them has raised entrepreneurial equity capital to fund its growth – in several cases even from the same VC investors that had previously funded then-fledgling start-ups such as Apple and Google, which have developed into major organisations that have had a transformative impact on the world economy.[1]

Young entrepreneurial companies are therefore an important part of today's knowledge-based economies, contributing to productivity growth, creating jobs, providing radical innovations and challenging established incumbents (Block et al., 2017 and 2018 a). Unfortunately, however, their funding is not as straightforward as the examples mentioned above may suggest (Denis, 2004). Specifically, capital for early-stage companies is scarce, and many entrepreneurs face challenges in funding their ventures, as early-stage companies are difficult to finance (Amit et al., 1998; Berger and Udell, 1998; Cressy, 2002; Cassar, 2004; Hall and Lerner, 2010). These difficulties arise because entrepreneurial ventures have highly uncertain prospects, lack tangible assets that financiers could use as collateral, and additionally pose severe information problems for financiers dealing with them (Amit et al., 1998; Hall and Lerner, 2010). Thus, despite the emergence of specialised entrepreneurial equity investors such as VC investors and business angels, early-stage companies' funding challenges often lead to financing constraints that limit their growth and might even force them out of business (Binks and Ennew, 1996; Carpenter and Petersen, 2002;

---

1 For example, the VC firm Sequoia Capital has funded Google and Apple, as well as Instagram, WhatsApp and AirBnB; similarly, the VC firm Kleiner Perkins (formerly Kleiner, Perkins, Caufield & Byers) has funded Google, Spotify and Uber (Chapman, 2018; Sequoia, 2019).

17

Cressy, 2002; Cosh et al., 2009). Consequently, entrepreneurial finance research that deals with early-stage companies' fundraising and investors' capital allocation is at the core of entrepreneurship research (Buchner et al., 2017).

However, the shortage of entrepreneurial funding varies by region, and it is more pressing in some regions than in others. In Europe, for example, the VC industry is significantly less developed than in the United States (US), as the sum of all VC investments as a share of gross domestic product (GDP) is only around 25% of that in the US (Kelly, 2011; Guerini and Quas, 2016).Therefore, it has been argued that a functioning pan-European VC market would be a vital prerequisite to securing the long-term competitiveness of the European Union (Grilli and Murtinu, 2014).

Given early-stage companies' funding challenges and their importance for overall economic growth and innovation (Kortum and Lerner, 2000; Samila and Sorenson, 2011; Block et al., 2017), governmental institutions and policymakers around the globe, and particularly in Europe, aim at closing the gap in early-stage entrepreneurial capital (Grilli and Murtinu, 2014; Block et al., 2018 a). Governments have traditionally responded by granting financial support to innovative companies, as well as intervening in the private VC sector or by setting up dedicated governmental VC firms to invest in promising start-up companies (Grilli and Murtinu, 2014; Guerini and Quas, 2016). Nonetheless, the funding gap persists, and new sources of capital that could help provide additional funding are thus sought after (Cressy, 2002; Denis, 2004; Block et al., 2018 a). Fortunately, however, innovation does not stop at the financing of start-ups either: various new types of financing and investors have developed in recent years, and these innovations may thus help close the funding gap (Bruton et al., 2015; Drover et al., 2017; Block et al., 2018 a).

Among recent funding innovations, equity crowdfunding is particularly interesting to evaluate, as proponents from academia and practice argue that it could complement or even replace traditional VC and BA funding (Agrawal et al., 2014; Ahlers et al., 2015; Goldman Sachs, 2015; Vulkan et al., 2016; Dushnitsky and Zunino, 2018). With equity crowdfunding, an entrepreneur raises capital through an online platform from a large number of typically small investors (the 'crowd'), who each contribute a small amount (Belleflamme et al., 2014; Mollick, 2014; Ahlers et al., 2015). By digitising the funding process and addressing small investors rather than venture capitalists or business angels, equity crowdfunding could unleash massive additional funding volumes for the financing of entrepreneurship (Agrawal et al., 2014; Ahlers et al., 2015). Fred Wilson, a prominent venture capitalist, estimates that if Americans contributed 1% of their in-vestable assets to crowdfunding, an additional USD 300 billion in funding would become available to the start-up ecosystem (Colao, 2012; The Economist, 2012).

However, big fundraising potential alone is not sufficient to make equi-ty crowdfunding a sustainable funding option for entrepreneurs and an at-tractive investment for crowdfunders. To assess whether equity crowdfund-ing could indeed sustainably help close the funding gap, it is important to understand how it shapes companies' subsequent development compared to traditional sources of funding. This is because investors' impact on ear-ly-stage companies' development and performance can be profound (Schwienbacher, 2013) and evidence suggests that VC investors add value to their portfolio companies by causally improving their performance be-yond providing capital (Chemmanur et al., 2011; Croce et al., 2013). Thus, to be a truly viable funding alternative for early-stage start-ups, equity crowdfunding must not imply a competitive disadvantage for companies.

But assessing how using equity crowdfunding as a funding source influ-ences companies' subsequent performance is not only of practical impor-tance for regulators and entrepreneurs, but also of great scholarly interest. Specifically, investors' impact on their portfolio companies is at the heart of entrepreneurial finance literature (Croce et al., 2013; Grilli and Murt-inu, 2014; Kerr et al., 2014; Dutta and Folta, 2016) and thus an understand-ing of new funding types, such as equity crowdfunding, is an important frontier of entrepreneurial finance research (Bruton et al., 2015). More-over, the nascent literature on crowdfunding (e.g., Agrawal et al., 2014; Mollick, 2014; Stanko and Henard, 2017; Signori and Vismara, 2018) lacks a commensurate analysis and would thus benefit from this examination as well.

Therefore, the *first overarching topic*[2] that this dissertation explores is the impact of equity crowdfunding on companies' post-funding performance, which is an important factor for the viability of equity crowdfunding as an alternative funding mechanism for early-stage ventures.

But while the examination of new players and funding forms is an im-portant research frontier, venture capitalists' investment approach and their impact on portfolio companies requires further scholarly attention, too. The question whether VC investors add value to their portfolio com-panies beyond providing capital, or just invest in superior companies, has

---

2 Please note that the specific research questions of this dissertation are derived in more detail in Chapter 2.2.

attracted scholarly interest for years (e.g., Gompers and Lerner, 2001; Baum and Silverman, 2004; Chemmanur et al., 2011; Croce et al., 2013) and it remains a hot topic in entrepreneurial finance research to date (Tykvová, 2018). Although recent research has provided evidence suggesting that the observed superior performance of VC-backed companies can at least partially be ascribed to the value-adding contributions of VC investors, there is mixed evidence suggesting that VC investors select companies with greater inherent development potential (called 'selection effect' or 'screening effect') (Chemmanur et al., 2011; Puri and Zarutskie, 2012; Croce et al., 2013).

However, little is known about potential heterogeneity among VC investors with respect to selection and treatment effects, as current research is typically limited to comparisons of different VC types such as independent venture capital (IVC), governmental venture capital (GVC) or corporate venture capital (CVC) investors (e.g., Park and Steensma, 2012; Chemmanur et al., 2014; Grilli and Murtinu, 2014; Guerini and Quas, 2016), and provides little evidence regarding other important VC investor characteristics. Hence, additional analyses are warranted to provide a more granular picture (Tykvová, 2018). However, a more detailed understanding of those VC investor characteristics that affect selection and treatment effects is not only of academic interest for the literature on screening and value-added in entrepreneurial equity financing (e.g., Gompers and Lerner, 2001; Baum and Silverman, 2004; Chemmanur et al., 2011; Croce et al., 2013; Kerr et al., 2014). It is also of significant practical relevance. Specifically, a more granular understanding of the contingencies of investor screening and value-added will enable more specific interventions by regulators and is of great importance to entrepreneurs, who seek valuable investor support. Accordingly, the *second major topic* of this dissertation is a better understanding of investor characteristics that cause heterogeneity in selection and treatment effects in VC financing. To assess this second major topic holistically, this dissertation also considers the relationship between investors' characteristics and their deal structuring practices, as the syndication of deals is closely related to investors' deal selection process and capabilities.

1.2 Structure of the Dissertation

The remainder of this dissertation is structured as follows. Chapter 2 provides an overview of the theoretical background as well as the extant research on entrepreneurial equity financing, and derives the research questions in detail. The third chapter is dedicated to answering the first research question and evaluates differences in the value-adding contributions of traditional investors and equity crowdfunders. Chapter 4 tackles the second research question and deals with the effect of industry specialisation, which is an important investor characteristic, on VC investors' investment selection and value-adding performance. Chapter 5 addresses the third research question and evaluates how investor–company-fit shapes VC syndication in Europe. Chapter 6 provides an overarching conclusion and discusses the theoretical and practical contribution of this dissertation.

2 Theoretical Background and Development of Research Questions

This chapter starts with a brief summary of the relevant theoretical background in Section 2.1 and then reviews the extant literature to derive the research questions of this dissertation in Section 2.2. To avoid redundancies, Section 2.1 focuses on the most relevant theoretical foundations and sets the stage for the subsequent passage, whereas Section 2.2 discusses the more recent literature and its gaps to derive the research questions.

2.1 Theoretical Background

Young entrepreneurial companies are an important part of today's knowledge-based economies, as they contribute to productivity growth, create jobs, provide radical innovations and challenge established incumbents (Block et al., 2017 and 2018 a). However, these companies often face financial constraints, as they are particularly difficult to finance (Amit et al., 1998; Denis, 2004; Hall and Lerner, 2010).

The funding challenge arises because entrepreneurial ventures have highly uncertain prospects, lack tangible assets that financiers could use as collateral, and additionally pose severe information problems for financiers dealing with them (Amit et al., 1998; Hall and Lerner, 2010). The 'asymmetric information' problem is particularly large for innovative entrepreneurial ventures, because the entrepreneur typically possesses better information about the success probability of her project than potential investors, for whom it is very challenging to evaluate the project's quality and expected value from the outside (Amit et al., 1998; Denis, 2004; Hall and Lerner, 2010). This kind of 'hidden information' problem is a common feature in many situations of economic life and especially corporate finance (Denis, 2004), as it occurs whenever one party to a transaction possesses information not known to the other party and is incentivised to exploit this informational advantage through misreporting (Amit et al., 1998). However, the 'hidden information' problem is particularly strong for entrepreneurial finance, given the immature state of development of the ventures to be funded (Carpenter and Petersen, 2002; Denis, 2004). Therefore, when funding entrepreneurial ventures, investors typically demand a particularly high premium to compensate for their risk of funding low-quality projects, often referred to as a 'lemons premium' (Carpenter and Petersen, 2002; Hall and Lerner, 2010) following Akerlof's (1970) seminal work on information asymmetries in the market for automobiles. In extreme, information asymmetries could make the market for innovative projects disappear, and it is widely held that information asymmetries lead to suboptimal investment levels (Akerlof, 1970; Amit et al., 1998; Denis, 2004; Hall and Lerner, 2010).

There are two paradigmatic responses to this challenge. On the one hand, public policymakers in many countries have responded by providing financial support to innovative companies using structured programs (such as the Horizon 2020 program of the European Commission), to fund innovation by entrepreneurial ventures (Hall and Lerner, 2010; Grilli and Murtinu, 2014; Block et al., 2018 a). On the other hand, in many countries, an ecosystem of specialist entrepreneurial equity investors has emerged, which are better able to overcome information asymmetries than other financial intermediaries: venture capitalists are the primary and most suitable source of capital fuelling innovation (Chan, 1983; Amit et al., 1998; Hall and Lerner, 2010; Croce et al., 2013; Drover et al., 2017).[3]

Due to the significant information asymmetries described, but also due to the highly dynamic nature of the young companies to be funded, many venture capitalists have adopted a standard best-practice investment process, which was first delineated by Tyebjee and Bruno (1984). The investment process consists of deal origination, deal screening and evaluation, deal structuring, and post-investment activities (Tyebjee and Bruno, 1984) and it is ideally terminated by an exit (Gorman and Sahlman, 1989). While the deal origination process serves to identify those ventures that shall be considered as investment prospects, these investment prospects are subsequently reviewed, and the more promising ones are evaluated in more detail to identify potentially successful ventures (Tyebjee and Bruno, 1984). The process and decision-making criteria that investors use to identify successful ventures has been of scholarly interest since the early days of VC re-

---

3 Besides venture capitalists, business angels and, more recently, crowdfunders and accelerators are also important sources of funding. However, venture capitalists have attracted by far the most research attention and thus many of the theoretical foundations of the broader literature on early-stage entrepreneurial equity financing have been established by venture capital research (Drover et al., 2017). Therefore, to outline the theoretical foundations, this section focuses on the characteristics of VC investors, and highlights the differences to other investor types as needed.

search (Drover et al., 2017). For instance, Tyebjee and Bruno (1984) and MacMillan et al. (1987) identified that factors such as market attractiveness, product differentiation, managerial capabilities and competition are important factors for venture capitalists' investment decisions. However, as Drover et al. (2017) point out, more recent research, for example by Petty and Gruber (2010), Kirsch et al. (2009) and Gompers et al. (2016 a) advance this view by highlighting that VC decision-making is a more complex and contingent process in which time-variant decision criteria are applied. Thus, although the findings of both Gompers et al. (2016 a) and Bernstein et al. (2017) suggest that characteristics of the founding team are likely to be the single most important criterion for VCs' investment decisions, a significant share of investors' decision-making remains shrouded in legend. This is to some extent a consequence of the fact that investors invest extremely selectively: according to evidence reported by Gompers et al. (2016 a), only 1 in 100 investment opportunities is eventually funded.

However, once a VC firm has decided that it would like to invest in a given venture, the investment terms need to be negotiated with the entrepreneur and potential syndicate partners in order to execute the deal (Tyebjee and Bruno, 1984; Bygrave, 1987). When structuring the deal, investors make extensive use of contractual provisions to discipline entrepreneurs and address the particularly strong 'moral hazard' problem: the risk that entrepreneurs will misallocate funds provided by venture capitalists for their own benefit (Amit et al., 1998; Denis, 2004). Because of the particularly strong moral hazard problem, venture capitalists have adopted commensurate contractual solutions that differ from those used in the traditional corporate finance context of larger, more established corporations (Denis, 2004). For instance, venture capitalists typically demand extensive and disproportionate control and cash flow rights, board seats, and liquidation rights, and provide monetary investment in a graduated, staged approach to monitor and incentivise entrepreneurs (Sahlman, 1990; Gompers, 1995; Kaplan and Strömberg, 2003). Consequently, these financing contracts reduce venture capitalists' risk and eventually shift it to the entrepreneur (Denis, 2004).

After the investment is completed, venture capitalists engage in extensive post-investment activities. For instance, Gorman and Sahlman (1989) report that venture capitalists spend about half of their time on portfolio work. As part of this portfolio work, venture capitalists' closely monitor their portfolio companies, making use of their strong control rights and board seats (Admati and Pfleiderer, 1994; Gompers, 1995; Lerner, 1995). Through close monitoring, investors are able to detect potential problems

(Mitchell et al., 1997) and reduce the agency cost from potential 'moral hazard' (Jensen and Meckling, 1976; Amit et al., 1998; Ueda, 2004). However, venture capitalists not only adopt a monitoring stance, but also take a collaborative approach (Tyebjee and Bruno, 1984), act as 'coaches' for their portfolio companies (Colombo and Grilli, 2010), and provide their portfolio companies with extensive support, for example through financial and strategic advice and support in management recruitment (Gorman and Sahlman, 1989; Sahlman, 1990; Sapienza et al., 1996; Hellmann and Puri, 2002; Sørensen, 2007). Through their support, venture capitalists augment the set of resources available to their portfolio companies, which, according to the resource-based view, is a determinant of company performance (Barney, 1991; Ireland et al., 2003; Croce et al., 2013). Consequently, several researchers have advanced theoretical arguments that the non-financial services provided by venture capitalists can enhance company performance (Casamatta, 2003; Ueda, 2004; Chemmanur et al., 2011).

However, due to the outlined peculiarities of the VC investment process – namely large information asymmetries, an extensive screening process with a very low acceptance rate, and investors' active post-investment behaviour – the question whether VC investors 'add value' (i.e. *cause* performance improvements) to their portfolio companies, or whether they are simply good at selecting high-potential ventures (so-called 'selection effect' or 'screening effect' (Croce et al., 2013)), is difficult to answer empirically and thus has been at the core of entrepreneurial finance research for years (see e.g., Gompers and Lerner, 2001; Baum and Silverman; 2004; Chemmanur et al., 2011; Croce et al., 2013). Today, a deeper understanding of selection and treatment effects is still warranted (Tykvová, 2018). However, this deeper understanding of selection and treatment effects is needed not only for venture capitalists. Given the emergence of new investor types such as crowdfunders and accelerators, it is vital to understand their impact on ventures they fund, too (Drover et al., 2017; Block et al., 2018 a).

Therefore, this dissertation is dedicated to a more thorough investigation of the selection and treatment effects for venture capitalists and new investor types, as well as the relationship between investor characteristics, screening and deal structuring. The next section presents a detailed review of the extant and more recent literature in this field, and derives the corresponding research questions the dissertation shall answer.

2.2 Literature Review and Development of Research Questions

2.2.1 Investor Value-added in Equity Crowdfunding

The question whether VC investors add value to their portfolio companies beyond providing capital, or simply select superior companies, has been part of the scientific discourse of entrepreneurial finance research for years (see e.g., Gompers and Lerner, 2001; Baum and Silverman; 2004; Chemmanur et al., 2011; Croce et al., 2013) and remains a topic that compels research interest (Tykvová, 2018).

In recent years, research has made significant progress towards answering this question due to new datasets and advanced empirical methodologies. Using US census data, Chemmanur et al. (2011) find evidence for a selection effect: VC investors invest in companies that are more productive and possess more human capital. Nonetheless, the authors also find evidence suggesting that VC investors are able to improve the efficiency of their portfolio companies. Leveraging a different US census dataset, Puri and Zarutskie (2011) find that VC-backed companies exhibit stronger revenue growth than matched, non-backed peers and conclude that VC investors add value by stimulating growth in their portfolio companies. Bertoni et al. (2011) and Croce et al. (2013) study similar research questions in the European context. Croce et al. (2013), in contrast to Chemmanur et al. (2011), do not find evidence for differences in productivity growth prior to the receipt of VC financing (i.e. no selection effect), but report a significant treatment effect that 'imprints' the portfolio companies such that the higher productivity growth is maintained even after a VC exits. Similarly, Bertoni et al. (2011) do not find any evidence for a selection effect, and report that investments from venture capitalists trigger strong employment and sales growth in new technology-based companies. Finally, Bernstein et al. (2016) use the introduction of new airline flight routes as an exogenous source of variation in VC monitoring to show empirically that reduced cost for monitoring by venture capitalists, and their resulting stronger involvement, leads to a performance increase of their portfolio companies, as reflected in more innovation and a higher probability of successful exits.

Building on the initial contributions on IVCs (e.g., Bertoni et al., 2011; Chemmanur et al., 2011; Puri and Zarutskie, 2011; Croce et al., 2013), scholars have started to push the boundaries of this research stream by investigating additional investor types to create an understanding of their value-adding contributions. For example, comparing GVCs and IVCs in

Europe, Grilli and Murtinu (2014) find that IVCs have a significant positive impact on the sales growth of their portfolio companies, while GVCs only provide a negligible value-adding effect. Chemmanur et al. (2014) find that ventures backed by CVCs are more innovative but less profitable than those companies funded by IVCs, which – according to the authors – suggests that these ventures may benefit from greater industry knowledge of their investors and that CVCs may be less sensitive to failure. Regarding business angels, Kerr et al. (2014) provide robust evidence that financing by angel groups is associated with greater likelihood of survival and greater operating performance. Moreover, Dutta and Folta (2016) are the first to compare the value-adding performance of venture capitalists and business angels, and find that the different kinds of investors contribute equally to innovation rates, but venture capital-backed companies achieve faster commercialisation in the form of successful exits (initial public offerings (IPOs) or acquisitions).

Lately, crowdfunding has emerged as an increasingly important financing alternative to VC and business angels (Mollick, 2014; Bruton et al., 2015; Drover et al., 2017; Block et al., 2018 a). With crowdfunding, an entrepreneur raises capital from a large number of investors (the 'crowd') who each contribute a small amount. The contributions of the crowd come typically in one of four forms: as a donation ('donation crowdfunding'), as a pre-order of a product ('reward-based crowdfunding'), as a credit ('lending crowdfunding'), or in exchange for a share of equity ('equity crowdfunding') (Belleflamme et al., 2014; Mollick, 2014; Ahlers et al., 2015). Donation crowdfunding is better suited for certain arts and humanitarian projects, as it resembles charitable giving, and lending crowdfunding is rarely accessible to start-ups due to their lack of credit history (Mollick, 2014). Thus, reward-based and equity crowdfunding are the predominant types of crowdfunding adopted by start-ups (Belleflamme et al., 2014). Moreover, some researchers even see equity crowdfunding as an alternative form of financing that has the potential to compete with traditional VC and BA financing (Vulkan et al., 2016; Dushnitsky and Zunino, 2018).

However, in extant research both equity crowdfunding as a funding type and the value-adding contributions of crowd investors in general are still underexplored (Dushnitsky and Zunino, 2018). Instead, prior research on crowdfunding addresses primarily signalling in and success drivers of crowdfunding campaigns (e.g., Ahlers et al., 2015; Colombo et al., 2015) as well as the decision-making and motivations of crowdfunders (e.g., Mollick and Ramana, 2016; Kuppuswamy and Bayus, 2017).

Although a nascent stream of research examines the post-funding performance of equity-crowdfunded companies (Hornuf et al., 2018; Signori and Vismara, 2018), none of these works allows for causal inferences about how the value-adding contributions of equity crowdfunding investors compare to those of venture capitalists or business angels. That is because none of the works compare equity-crowdfunded companies to their 'counterfactuals' – matched peers that used alternative funding sources.

This is an important gap to close, as it would extend the literature on investor value-added that at present considers different types of venture capitalists and business angels (e.g., Croce et al., 2013; Grilli and Murtinu, 2014; Kerr et al., 2014; Dutta and Folta, 2016) to equity crowdfunding. Second, it would add to the literature on crowdfunding (e.g., Agrawal et al., 2014; Mollick, 2014; Stanko and Henard, 2017; Signori and Vismara, 2018), as understanding crowdfunding's influence on companies' subsequent development is critical for this research stream (Stanko and Henard, 2017; Dushnitsky and Zunino, 2018).

Finally, from a rather practical standpoint, the question as to how equity crowdfunding impacts companies' subsequent performance is a decisive factor determining whether or not equity crowdfunding will be able to establish itself as a viable funding alternative to VC and BA funding – which could help close the funding gap and provide much-needed capital to fund entrepreneurial ventures (Block et al., 2018 a). Therefore, the first research question is formulated as follows:

Research Question 1: How does equity crowdfunding investors' value-added to portfolio companies compare to traditional early-stage investors' value-added?

2.2.2 Specialisation, Screening and Value-added

While an understanding of new investor types is an important frontier of entrepreneurial finance research, 'traditional' venture capitalists' screening and value-added also calls for further scholarly attention. As discussed in Section 2.2.1, recent research has delivered evidence that the observed superior performance of VC-backed companies is at least in part causally driven by the value-adding contributions of VC investors, but there is mixed evidence suggesting that VC investors select companies with greater inherent development potential (called the 'screening effect') (Chemmanur et al., 2011; Puri and Zarutskie; 2012; Croce et al., 2013). Moreover, recent research on VC screening and value-added focuses on differences among investor types, such as IVCs, GVCs, and CVCs (Park and Steensma,

2012; Chemmanur et al., 2014; Grilli and Murtinu, 2014; Guerini and Quas, 2016). Besides that, very little is known about how certain investor attributes influence venture capitalists' ability to select high-potential ventures and add value to them (Tykvová, 2018). One exception is the work by Krishnan et al. (2011), who find that more reputable investors select higher-quality companies, but their reputation nonetheless has a significant value-adding effect on their post-IPO performance.

Nonetheless, deeper knowledge of the antecedents of investors' selection and value-adding capabilities is scarce, and there is little empirical evidence that helps identify and explain heterogeneity among investors regarding these factors. Therefore, it is necessary to derive a more detailed understanding that considers the heterogeneity of selection and treatment effects among investors with varying characteristics (Tykvová, 2018).

For instance, the contribution of investors' specialised industry expertise as a potential antecedent for selection and value-added is underexplored. While specialisation (vs. diversification) as a VC investment strategy has been studied by prior research (Gompers et al., 2009; Knill, 2009; Buchner et al., 2017), its effects on investors' selection and value-adding capabilities as well as for the performance of portfolio companies are not well understood. This is due to several shortcomings, such as improper handling of endogeneity, coarse and potentially biased performance metrics, and suboptimal specialisation measures that do not account for the fit (Lungeanu and Zajac, 2016) between investors' specialised expertise and the focal venture (discussed in detail in Section 4.1.2). However, it seems highly probable that venture capitalists' specialised expertise affects their selection and value-adding capabilities. For instance, greater specialised expertise may reduce information asymmetries (Gompers et al., 2009) or allow investors to provide their portfolio companies with better guidance during the post-investment collaboration (Norton and Tenenbaum, 1993). However, a diverse knowledge stock may bring advantages for VC investors' portfolio work too (Matusik and Fitza, 2012), such that a more thorough analytical and empirical investigation is required to shed light on this relationship.

Therefore, further research is warranted that unites the research stream on VC specialisation with that on VC selection and value-added by investigating the influence of VC investors' specialised expertise on their ability to select high-potential ventures and improve their performance. This type of research would advance the literature on selection and value-added in VC (e.g., Chemmanur et al., 2011; Puri and Zarutskie; 2012; Croce et al., 2013) by contributing to a more detailed understanding of potential heterogeneity among investors with varying characteristics. Furthermore, it can add to the literature on specialisation as a VC investment strategy (e.g., Gompers et al., 2009; Knill, 2009; Buchner et al., 2017). Moreover, a more thorough understanding of venture capitalists' selection would also be beneficial for the literature on VC decision-making (e.g., Kirsch et al., 2009; Petty and Gruber, 2011), given that systematic evidence on venture capitalists' selection processes is very scarce (Bernstein et al., 2015). Hence, the second research question of this dissertation is the following:

Research Question 2: How does venture capitalists' industry specialisation affect their ability to select high-potential ventures and add value to them?

2.2.3 Specialisation and VC Syndication

As part of the deal-structuring process (Tyebjee and Bruno, 1984), venture capitalists often form syndicates in which multiple venture capitalists jointly invest in a funding round (Bygrave, 1987), which makes syndication one of the characteristic features of the VC industry (Wright and Lockett, 2003; Ferrary, 2010). Recent empirical research has investigated VC syndication from various perspectives, focusing on syndicate composition and dynamics, for instance with respect to the formation of long-term syndicate networks and their relationship with investors' status and reputation (Hopp and Lukas, 2014; Hochberg et al., 2015; Milanov and Shepherd, 2013; Gompers et al., 2016b) as well as the effect of syndication on investment outcomes (Das et al., 2011; Tian, 2012).

But there is a fundamental aspect of VC syndication for which empirical evidence is scarce: namely, lead investors' decisions and motivations to initiate the formation of a syndicate for a particular deal as well as the antecedents of this decision (Jääskeläinen, 2012). Given that only around 40%–50% of the deals in European VC markets are actually syndicated (Wright and Lockett, 2003), and considering that the investor who originates the deal eventually decides whether or not to invite co-investors to join the syndicate (Lerner, 1994; De Clercq and Dimov, 2004; Manigart et al., 2006) it is crucial to establish a more fine-grained understanding of the driving forces for investors' decisions to share a particular investment opportunity with co-investors and to undertake others individually. Although there is a fair amount of theory on the different general motives for syndication, such as portfolio diversification, risk reduction or future deal-flow generation through reciprocity with other investors (e.g., Lockett and Wright, 2001; Manigart et al., 2006; Jääskeläinen, 2012; Manigart and Wright, 2013), these theoretical arguments have received little empirical scrutiny and extant research cannot explain investors' decisions to syndicate at the deal level. Put differently, current theory does not reliably allow us to predict which deals a VC investor will syndicate and which ones the VC investor will complete individually.

However, prior research (Manigart et al., 2006; Casamatta and Haritchabalet, 2007; Gompers et al., 2009) provides theoretical arguments that specialised industry expertise might be beneficial for investors' investment selection, as it may reduce information asymmetries for investors and it is widely held that syndication is also a means to reduce risk for investors through collaboration of investors in evaluating risky deals (Lerner, 1994; Brander et al., 2002; Manigart et al., 2006; Manigart and Wright, 2013; Lockett and Wright, 2001; Jääskeläinen, 2012).

Therefore, it is worthwhile to investigate empirically how VC investor specialisation and the fit between their expertise and the focal venture influence VC investors' decisions to form a syndicate. Moreover, since VC investors trade resources when syndicating (Hochberg et al., 2015), it is also valuable to assess the influence of investor–company-fit and specialised expertise on the attractiveness of potential syndicate partners. Such research could advance the literature on VC syndication (e.g., Manigart et al., 2006; Hochberg et al., 2015) and VC decision-making (Kirsch et al., 2009; Petty and Gruber, 2011) by providing a fine-grained, empirically-based understanding of lead investors' decisions and motivations to syndicate at the deal level. Moreover, this analysis would contribute to the literature on specialisation (vs. diversification) as VC investment strategy (e.g., Gompers et al., 2009; Matusik and Fitza, 2012; Buchner et al., 2017) by linking it with the literature on syndication and thus alluding to the operational consequences of investors' specialisation strategy, which is an important factor of VC heterogeneity. Consequently, the third research question of this dissertation is:

Research Question 3: How does venture capitalists' industry specialisation affect the formation and composition of syndicates?

3 How to Digitise Investor Value-added? A Comparison of Investor Value-added in Equity Crowdfunding and Traditional Early-stage Financing

This first essay intends to explore differences in the value-adding contributions of traditional investors (venture capitalists and business angels) and equity crowdfunding investors to address Research Question 1.[4] The first section, 3.1, reviews the literature, and Section 3.2 derives the hypotheses. Section 3.3. elaborates on the dataset, variables, and sample construction. Section 3.4 presents the empirical analyses and results. Section 3.5 presents a discussion of the results and the limitations of this research. Finally, Section 6 sets forth the conclusions.

3.1 Literature Review

3.1.1 Literature on Crowdfunding

Until recently, start-up companies in their early stages typically had to rely on VC investors and business angels to fund their growing ventures. Now,

---

4 This chapter is largely based on a joint working paper with Professor Carolin Bock (Technische Universität Darmstadt) and is thus written from the first-person-plural point of view (i.e., *we*) in order to indicate that the research also reflects the opinions of the co-author. The working paper has been presented at three conferences and a 6-page abridged version entitled 'Is equity-crowdfunding a market for lemons? – An empirical investigation of early-stage startups' performance' has been accepted for publication in the 2018 edition of *Frontiers of Entrepreneurship Research BCERC Proceedings* (forthcoming). The conference contributions are: (1) Bock, Carolin; Tatomir, Simon (2018): 'Is equity-crowdfunding a market for lemons? – An empirical investigation of early-stage startups' performance'; Babson BCERC, Waterford Institute of Technology, Waterford, Ireland. (2) Bock, Carolin; Tatomir, Simon (2018): 'No wisdom of the crowd? – Why early-stage firms choose equity crowdfunding and how it impacts their performance'; Interdisziplinäre Jahreskonferenz Entrepreneurship, Innovation und Mittelstand („G-Forum"), Stuttgart; (3) Bock, Carolin; Tatomir, Simon (2017): 'Is equity-crowdfunding a market for lemons? An empirical investigation of equity-crowdfunded startups' performance'; Interdisziplinäre Jahreskonferenz Entrepreneurship, Innovation und Mittelstand („G-Forum"), Wuppertal.

start-ups can make use of crowdfunding as an increasingly important financing alternative to raise capital from a large number of investors (the 'crowd') who each contribute a smaller amount (e.g., Belleflamme et al., 2014; Mollick, 2014; Bruton et al., 2015).

As mentioned in Section 2.2.1, extant research on crowdfunding devoted little attention to both equity crowdfunding as a funding type and the value-adding contributions of crowd investors in general (Dushnitsky and Zunino, 2018). Instead, research on crowdfunding addresses primarily the signalling of crowdfundees and the success drivers of crowdfunding campaigns (Ahlers et al., 2015; Colombo et al., 2015; Moss et al., 2015; Lukkarinen et al., 2016; Manning and Bejarano, 2017) as well as the decision-making behaviour and motivations of crowdfunders (Cholakova and Clarysse, 2015; Mollick and Ramana, 2016; Vismara, 2016; Kuppuswamy and Bayus, 2017).

Although a nascent stream of research examines the post-funding performance of equity-crowdfunded companies (Hornuf et al., 2018; Signori and Vismara, 2018), none of the existing works allow for causal inferences about the value-adding contributions of equity crowdfunding investors or comparisons to be made about its impact relative to other investor types, such as venture capitalists. For instance, Signori and Vismara (2018) analyse the outcomes of investments made via Crowdcube, the UK's largest equity crowdfunding platform, by monitoring the post-funding development of the equity-crowdfunded companies. Out of the 212 companies in the sample, 74 raised follow-on funding, 3 were acquired and 38 failed. In a similar vein, Hornuf et al. (2018) track the survival and follow-up funding of German and British start-up firms that ran at least one equity crowdfunding campaign. Hornuf et al. (2018) report that German equity-crowdfunded companies have a higher propensity to receive follow-on funding from business angels or venture capitalists, but also have a higher risk of failure than companies from the UK. Moreover, the authors identify company characteristics that are related to follow-on funding – for instance, the number of senior managers is positively related to follow-on funding, whereas company age at the time of the funding campaign exhibits a negative relationship to it.

However, none of these works compare equity-crowdfunded companies to their 'counterfactuals' (i.e. matched peers that used alternative funding sources). As such, it is not possible to make inferences about the causal impact of equity crowdfunding on the subsequent development of the firms. We address this gap and shed light on the value-adding services of crowdfunders and the outcomes for crowdfundees, by comparing the value-added by investors in equity crowdfunding with traditional early-stage financing (i.e. BA and VC financing). Assessing the value-adding contributions of 'the crowd' is an important step that will help us to better understand how innovative, digital platform-based funding mechanisms, such as equity crowdfunding, shape the performance of entrepreneurial companies (see Dushnitsky and Zunino, 2018; Stanko and Henard, 2017). The value of undertaking this exercise is twofold: first, the fact that platform-based start-up funding mechanisms form the basis of a new context for the value-adding services of investors necessitates revision and re-testing of the extant theory; and second, crowd investors are a new class of investors that differ from traditional investors and therefore, may add value in different ways. Thus, entrepreneurial finance research needs to disentangle the differences in value-adding activities amongst the growing number of funding alternatives and different investor types. This will facilitate understanding of the suitability of different investor types for entrepreneurs and start-ups based on their preferences and their stage of development (Dutta and Folta, 2016). Further, regulators can draw conclusions about whether they need to intervene if market forces are not balanced.

3.1.2 Literature on Traditional Investor's Value-added

Research on the value-added by early-stage investors has been at the heart of entrepreneurial finance literature for decades (e.g., Gorman and Sahlman, 1989; Sahlman, 1990; Gompers and Lerner, 2004; Ferrary and Granovetter, 2009). It is widely reported that early-stage investors provide potentially value-adding services to their portfolio companies in four areas (see Grilli and Murtinu, 2014 and Dutta and Folta, 2016 for a similar structuring).

First, in order to detect potential problems (Mitchell et al., 1997), to overcome information problems between investors and entrepreneurs (Amit et al., 1998; Ueda, 2004) and to reduce agency cost (Jensen and Meckling, 1976), traditional investors closely monitor their portfolio companies after the initial investment (Admati and Pfleiderer, 1994; Gompers, 1995; Lerner, 1995). To do so effectively, venture capitalists may take seats on the boards of the investments, stage the payout of their investments or negotiate control levers at a level that is disproportionate to their equity in the company (Sahlman, 1990; Gompers, 1995; Lerner, 1995; Kaplan and Strömberg, 2003).

Second, investors act as 'coaches' (Colombo and Grilli, 2010) and provide managerial support in the form of, for example, financial and strategic advice and may even support managerial recruitment (Gorman and Sahlman, 1989; Sahlman, 1990; Sapienza et al., 1996; Hellmann and Puri, 2002; Sørensen, 2007). In doing so, VCs augment and influence the resources available to their portfolio companies (Barney, 1991), which, according to the resource-based view, is a crucial factor that informs company success and performance (Ireland et al., 2003). Hence, current research on VC and private equity has established that both agency cost theory and the resource-based view complement one another in terms of explaining investor value-added (Meuleman et al., 2009; Croce et al., 2013). It is important to note that VC investors often specialise in certain industries and financing stages in order to perform their monitoring and coaching functions more effectively (Gupta and Sapienza, 1992; Norton and Tenenbaum, 1993). Moreover, spatial proximity is a key factor that influences monitoring (Tian, 2012) and managerial involvement. For instance, Tian (2012) finds that venture capitalists stage their funding more strongly when they invest in distant portfolio companies in order to monitor portfolio companies more easily and 'to keep the entrepreneur on a tight leash' (Tian, 2012, p. 136).

Third, VC investors and business angels provide their portfolio companies with access to their network of contacts, which may include other investors, potential partners, customers and suppliers (Hochberg et al., 2007; Werth and Boeert, 2013).

Finally, the funding and support provided by early-stage investors works as an endorsement which acts as a signal as to the quality of a portfolio company to external third parties. As a result, portfolio companies benefit from better access to external resources, such as partners (Hsu, 2006) and talent (Hellmann and Puri, 2002).

Taken together, the value-adding activities provided by VC investors and business angels have been found to have a causal impact on the performance of their portfolio companies.[5] For instance, Chemmanur et al. (2011) and Croce et al. (2013) report that VC investors improve the productivity and growth of their portfolio companies in both the US and Eu-

---

5 However, it is important to note that the relative importance (i.e. the respective *individual* contribution to value-added) of the different factors at play (monitoring, provision of managerial capabilities, access to networks, and endorsement) remain underexplored, as extant research has typically not been able to disentangle the effects (Manigart and Wright, 2013).

rope. Moreover, both Puri and Zarutskie (2011) and Bertoni et al. (2011) report that the value-adding activities from venture capitalists enhance employment and sales growth for their portfolio companies. Finally, Bernstein et al. (2016) show empirically that the reduced costs caused by the monitoring of venture capitalists and the resultant stronger involvement of investors leads to an increase in the performance of portfolio companies, typically in the form of increased innovation and a higher probability of a successful exit. With respect to business angels, Kerr et al. (2014) provide robust evidence that financing by angel groups is associated with a greater likelihood of survival and better operating performance, as reflected in higher levels of employment and more traffic on companies' websites. Moreover, Dutta and Folta (2016) compare the performance of venture capitalists and business angels in terms of value-added and find that both kinds of investors contribute equally to innovation rates, but that venture capital-backed companies achieve faster commercialisation via successful exits (in the form of IPOs or acquisitions).

3.2 Hypothesis Development

While the value-adding activities of traditional investors and their impact on venture performance has been the research object of several studies, evidence and theory about the value-adding services of crowdfunding investors have barely been explored in the extant literature (Dushnitsky and Zunino, 2018). In the following section, we provide a theoretical perspective on the value-adding services of equity crowdfunding investors in line with the four dimensions of impact outlined in the previous section, 3.1.2 (namely monitoring, provision of managerial competencies, access to network, and endorsement).

The *monitoring* of portfolio companies is inherently more challenging for equity crowdfunding investors than it is for traditional investors. First and foremost, due to contractual differences between angel and VC financing on one side and equity crowdfunding on the other, crowdfunders have very little control over or rights to the companies they invest in (Hornuf and Schwienbacher, 2014). As a result of the weaker control rights and the fact that ownership of crowdfunded companies is much more dispersed (due to the high number of small investors), crowdfunding investors are not typically able to take board seats to exert control. Moreover, the staging of these investments is less common. Finally, personal interactions are often not possible as geographic proximity, which is an important characteristic of many VC and angel investments, is reduced in the context of digital platform investing. Agrawal et al. (2015) find, for example, that the average distance between investors and artists on a crowdfunding platform dedicated to music is 5,000 km.

In terms of *managerial competencies*, 'the crowd' could potentially match the expertise provided by professional investors, with several works providing evidence of the often-cited 'wisdom of the crowd'. Based on their case study, which focuses on a crowdfunded IT start-up in France, Schwienbacher and Larralde (2010) report that many of the investors possess expertise relevant to the start-up, as many of the investors are, for example, professional search engine optimisers or IT or marketing experts. In their pioneering work on openness in the product crowdfunding context, Stanko and Henard (2017) show that crowdfundees' open search depth (that is, the intensity with which companies draw from external sources) enhances product market performance, suggesting that companies benefit from drawing more intensely from the expertise of their crowd investors. Mollick and Nanda (2016) assess the outcomes of crowdfunded theatre projects and find that projects backed by the crowd alone perform just as well as those selected by both experts and the crowd, suggesting that the crowd possesses critical expert knowledge. Besides, when we widen the focus beyond the literature on crowdfunding so that it encompasses other aspects of 'openness', we find numerous examples of successful crowd contributions to vital strategy and innovation processes in mature companies and organisations, suggesting that even established companies can benefit from contributions from the crowd and that emerging companies in their early stages could, therefore, benefit too (Matzler et al., 2014; Schlagwein and Bjørn-Andersen, 2014; Tavakoli et al., 2017).

However, even though the crowd of investors potentially possess the expertise required by start-ups and they are typically eager to contribute more than just funding to the start-up projects they invest in (Schwienbacher and Larralde, 2010),[6] it is challenging and costly for start-ups to manage such a large, dispersed and geographically distant group of investors (Agrawal et al., 2014). In principle, crowdfunded start-ups could ac-

---

6 However, there is evidence for an alternative standpoint, too. For instance, Cholakova and Clarysse (2015) find that non-financial motives (e.g., helping others) are not an important motivational driver for the use of equity crowdfunding. Moreover, Agrawal et al. (2014) also claim that equity crowdfunding investors are less likely to make an effort to contribute to the success of the startup due to their lower level of investment.

tively involve their investors in their strategy and innovation process by way of 'open strategy' processes that make use of digital platforms which stimulate and synthesise the input from a large group of stakeholders (e.g., Sailer et al., 2017; Tavakoli et al., 2017). The orchestration of such IT-enabled, open strategy and innovation processes is not trivial, however, and requires several preconditions to be met (Sailer et al., 2017). While equity crowdfunders are very likely to be able to contribute to open strategy processes due to their high IT-literacy and experience with technology (evidenced by their tendency to invest in novel business models via an online platform), the organisational preconditions for this contribution are typically absent as most equity-crowdfunded companies do not engage their crowd investors in strategy development on a regular and structured basis (potentially due to the substantial resources required) (Sailer et al., 2017)).

As a consequence, we conclude that, even though crowdfunding investors may have the capacity to provide managerial support, these resources remain largely inaccessible for the funded companies. The end result of this is that the *provision* of effective managerial support is significantly reduced where equity crowdfunding is relied on compared to in circumstances where VC or angel financing are used.

In terms of *access to networks*, crowd investors could potentially outperform traditional investors as a result of the sheer number of links to potential customers or partners possessed by the crowd. That being said, crowd investors certainly lack the connections to professional investors who are capable of facilitating successful funding in (larger) follow-on rounds (e.g., Bygrave, 1988; Agrawal, 2014). However, access to the network of equity crowdfunders is, like the access to their managerial competencies, blocked by the lack of structured channels which allow entrepreneurs to engage and manage their investor community in an effective manner. Consequently, the valuable social capital (Sorensen and Stuart, 2001; Hochberg et al., 2007; Werth and Boeert, 2013) present within the networks of crowd investors remains an unexploited resource for equity-crowdfunded ventures.

When evaluating the ability of equity crowdfunding investors to add value to their portfolio companies through *endorsement*, it is important to consider the role of reputation. While the provision of capital to a start-up is generally a positive signal to third parties, the value of the endorsement does vary depending on the source of capital (e.g., when comparing VC to public subsidies (Hsu, 2006)), with investor reputation being the key driver for certification (Timmons and Bygrave, 1986; Gompers, 1996; Hsu, 2004). In that regard, the average equity crowdfunding investor is likely to be less reputable than the average venture capitalist, as certain practitioners and scholars question the sophistication of crowd investors (Agrawal, 2014), with some even considering equity crowdfunding to be a 'funding source of last resort' (Ahlers et al., 2015).

Taken together, these considerations suggest that equity crowdfunding investors and traditional investors (venture capitalists and business angels) differ in their ability to add value to portfolio companies. Based on our review, we conclude that equity crowdfunding investors are likely to add less value to companies because they are not able to monitor portfolio companies closely, their (alleged) managerial competencies and their networks are largely inaccessible to portfolio companies, and they are less reputable.[7] Accordingly, we hypothesise:

Hypothesis 1: Equity crowdfunding has a causal negative impact on post-funding performance of start-ups compared to seed and angel financing.

However, before turning to the operationalisation of our hypothesis, we want to briefly highlight the role of the non-random matching of companies to investors (Tykvová, 2018) in the context of equity crowdfunding. Given that entrepreneurs choose the kind of funding for which they apply (i.e. if they aim to raise funds from business angels and VC investors, launch an equity crowdfunding campaign or even do so sequentially), it is possible that the quality of companies raising equity crowdfunding could be different to that of their VC and angel-backed peers. This is especially the case since one of the two funding options might be more attractive for companies with certain (performance-related) characteristics (Ahlers et al., 2015). Therefore, we need test for the presence of endogeneity explicitly and address it accordingly. Empirical evidence as to the presence of endogeneity and potential selection effects would then be an interesting starting point from which inferences could be drawn about the current accep-

---

7 Note that the relative weights of the different value-adding factors are currently unknown (Manigart and Wright, 2013). However, given that our review suggests traditional investors have superior value-adding capabilities compared to equity crowdfunders in all of the four categories (monitoring, provision of managerial competencies, access to networks, and endorsement), it follows that the *overall* value-adding effect of equity crowdfunding investors is lower than that of traditional investors. In similar vein, Dutta and Folta (2016) acknowledge that they are 'are unable to disentangle whether the value-added benefits are obtained from the primary effect of the investment (e.g., monitoring and governance) or through the secondary effect of the investment (e.g., signaling and information intermediation)' (Dutta and Folta, 2016, p. 43).

tance of equity crowdfunding as an alternative funding mechanism. We will thus touch on this point in our 'Results and Discussion' section.

3.3 Data and Research Methodology

3.3.1 Data Source

For our analyses, we use the Crunchbase dataset from 22 November 2016 and hand-collected information about company industry affiliation and social media footprint. Crunchbase is a database that provides information about new ventures and investments, and is operated by TechCrunch, an influential entrepreneurship website with good coverage of start-ups and established high-tech ventures. Crunchbase has been found to have broader coverage of VC investments than other databases that are commonly relied upon, such as Thomson One or Venture Source, as it covers a larger number of small investments (Kaminski et al., 2019). Given that the amounts invested during equity crowdfunding campaigns are often rather small compared to the universe of VC investments, Crunchbase's broad coverage is advantageous for our analysis. Not surprisingly, this rather novel dataset has gained increasing popularity with those undertaking entrepreneurship and finance research on VC (e.g., Block and Sandner, 2009; Alexy et al., 2012 Werth and Boeert, 2013; Croce et al., 2018) and in related fields, like marketing (Homburg et al., 2014). Our sample construction procedure will be discussed in Section 3.3.4, as our central variables must first be defined. We will therefore do so in the following section.

3.3.2 Dependent Variables

Our major goal is to compare the value-added by equity crowdfunding investors with that of traditional seed and early-stage investors along multiple dimensions, in order to obtain a more refined picture of the potential differences. To structure our work, we build on the related methodologies of Kerr et al. (2014) and Croce et al. (2018) and run analyses about the interim success, ultimate success, and growth and operations of the portfolio companies. Similar to these two studies, we track the interim success of companies using their ability to acquire further funding as the foundation for our assessment. We define ultimate success as a successful IPO or trade sale. Analyses about company size and growth complement these tests as they factor in more operational performance indicators.

To measure investors' impact on the interim success of companies, we use variables that capture the follow-on financing progress of companies. First, we use a dummy variable (*At least 1 follow-on round*) to measure whether companies have raised at least one subsequent financing round; second, we consider a variable that reflects the number of follow-on financing rounds that companies raise after the treatment round[8] (*Follow-on rounds*), as well as a variable that captures the natural logarithm of the amount of capital raised in subsequent funding rounds (*ln(Follow on total amount)*). All of these variables are derived from related research (Werth and Boeert, 2013; Kerr et al., 2014; Croce et al., 2018) and capture companies' interim success, because investors will, ceteris paribus, provide more follow-on financing to successful companies than to unsuccessful companies.

To measure the impact of investors on the ultimate success of a company, we employ a dummy variable (*IPO/Acquisition*), which indicates whether companies have been acquired or went public before our reference date. This variable is used in related research (e.g., Werth and Boeert, 2013; Kerr et al., 2014; Croce et al., 2018) to measure the ultimate success of start-ups, because it captures whether early-stage investors are able to 'cash out' (Croce et al., 2018).

To complement our analyses of companies' performance in terms of financing and ultimate success, we aim to assess investors' impact on companies' operating performance and growth as well. This assessment is particularly insightful, as a definition of performance that is too narrow – for instance, one which only considers follow-on financing – could be problematic if equity-crowdfunded start-ups' business models differ from seed or angel-financed companies in a way that reduces the necessity for follow-on investment. As argued by Kerr et al. (2014), one would ideally consider an array of performance variables (e.g., sales, product introductions), which is practically impossible because public data on young, private ventures is extremely scarce. To tackle data scarcity, Kerr et al. (2014) measure start-up growth and operating performance using employment levels and

---

8 The treatment round is the first equity crowdfunding round in case of equity crowdfunded firms and the corresponding (i.e. matched) seed or BA round. For further details, please refer to the detailed description of the matching procedure in Section 3.3.4.

growth in website visits. We build on their approach by assessing growth in company Facebook (fan page).

We use Facebook likes rather than website visits, because the importance of social media has increased significantly at the expense of traditional (corporate) websites since Kerr et al. (2014) started data collection in 2008. As a result of the growing impact of social media, a number of scholars have scrutinised its association with company success, and found positive associations. For instance, the literature finds a positive association between effective social media use and equity value (Chung et al., 2014), company legitimacy (Bapna and Benner, 2014), sales growth (Kumar et al., 2013), customer profitability (Rishika et al., 2013), and venture financing (Agrawal et al., 2012).

Overall, these findings provide sound evidence that the extent of a start-up's social media followership is associated positively with its performance and can therefore serve as a proxy for its performance. Building on the methodology of Kerr et al. (2014), we assess the number of likes of a start-up's page on Facebook at two points in time (March 2017 and July 2017) and consider the log ratio of the number of 'likes' across the two periods (*ln(Likes growth)*) as a proxy for their growth. By using growth in 'likes', rather than the absolute level of 'likes', we account for the fact that the absolute level varies depending on the business model and other start-up specific traits, as Kerr et al. (2014) point out with respect to website visits.

Additionally, we examine employment levels (*ln(Employees)*) using data from Crunchbase. As Crunchbase reports company employee counts in ranges (e.g., 10–50, 50–100), we transform the ranges into point estimates by applying a consistent rule to all ventures within the specified range. We replace the range by the median of each range and take its natural logarithm because the variable is skewed.

3.3.3 Independent Variables and Controls

Our central independent variable is a dummy variable (*ECF dummy*) that indicates whether a company has raised an equity crowdfunding investment round.

We control for company age to account for the fact that our dependent variables typically vary throughout the lifetime of a company. In addition, we control for the time that has passed between the focal funding round and our reference date to account for the fact that success, measured by our dependent variables, takes time to materialise. Moreover, we include founding year, funding year, industry, and country-fixed effects. The founding and funding year variables proxy for cyclicality in the availability of capital, as well as the overall economy, both of which affect company success. Industry-fixed effects control for a variety of differences among industries, such as capital requirements, competition, investor appetite, funding round size, and growth prospects. Crunchbase does not provide a unique industry for each company, but instead lists a varying and inconsistent array of categories for each company. Therefore, we manually map companies to one-digit SIC industries, thereby following related research that manually enriches the Crunchbase dataset with a more suitable industry definition (Homburg et al., 2014; Croce et al., 2018). Finally, country-fixed effects account for institutional and regulatory differences as well as differences in availability of capital.

3.3.4 Sample Construction and Matching Procedure

The construction of our sample follows a two-step procedure. First, we select equity-crowdfunded companies and potential peers from Crunchbase that are suited for our analysis, then we match equity-crowdfunded companies and their conventionally funded counterparts and retain only those observations for which the matching was successful.

In this first step, we identify companies founded between 2010 and 2014 that had an equity crowdfunding financing (the treatment group) or a seed or angel investment round (the control group) using Crunchbase. During a firm's early stages, classification of seed and angel rounds is unclear. Often, seed rounds also include investment from individual investors, and angel rounds may involve VC investors as well (Croce et al., 2016). Hence, we include both funding round types, in line with the approach used by Croce et al. (2018). The restriction of the sample period is due to the fact that equity crowdfunding gained significant traction only after 2010, following the foundation of some of today's leading equity crowdfunding platforms in the UK and US (Hurley, 2011; Huhman, 2012). Moreover, given our dependent variables, performance differences among companies become evident only after a certain period. Similar to Werth and Boeert (2013), we therefore restrict the sample to companies that have been founded sufficiently long before our reference date. We require the information needed for each analysis to be available, as we want to run all analyses with a consistent sample.

In the second step, we match equity-crowdfunded companies with their conventionally funded counterparts and retain those companies for which the matching was successful. As our performance variables are defined relative to a specific financing round (which we call treatment round), we need to select peers based on funding round characteristics. To do so, we begin with the first equity crowdfunding round of each company and match it with angel/seed rounds from the same country and industry, with a maximum absolute difference of half a year between the equity crowdfunding round and its peer concerning both the funding round date and the company founding date. We ensure that each company and each funding round is used only once in the sample. If a peer company matches more than one equity-crowdfunded company, we pair it with the company that has the closest funding date. This procedure is required because multiple observations from the same company could potentially bias the regression results. This process results in a final sample comprised of 588 equity-crowdfunded ventures and 6,808 peers.

3.3.5 Empirical Methodology

To examine our hypotheses, we run several types of multivariate regression. We begin with ordinary least squares (OLS) regressions. We perform the Breusch-Pagan (1979) test for heteroscedasticity and use robust standard errors as a response. Moreover, we use the two-step Heckman (1979) correction in our regressions of *ln(Likes growth)*, to account for the fact that we observe the dependent variable only for a (potentially non-random) subsample.

However, since we hypothesise that equity-crowdfunded company quality and peer quality may differ and may affect both company financing choice and subsequent performance, we need to address endogeneity explicitly in order to avoid the possibility that omitted variable bias resulting from unobserved self-selection processes drives our results (see, for example, Hamilton and Nickerson, 2003). Hence, we test for endogeneity of our *ECF dummy* by using differences in Sargan-Hansen statistics, a procedure that is robust to heteroscedasticity and, thus, more reliable for our case than, for example, the more widely used Durbin-Wu-Hausman test (Baum et al., 2003). Whenever we find our *ECF dummy* variable to be endogenous, we employ IV regressions (see, for example, Bascle, 2008 for an extensive overview). If we do not find evidence of endogeneity, we use OLS regressions, since OLS is more efficient than IV regressions (e.g., Baum et al., 2003).

As an aside, the Heckman correction (Heckman, 1974 and 1979) is also frequently used to control for endogeneity from self-selection (see Tucker, 2010 for an introduction and Saboo et al., 2016 for examples). However, the results reported by Certo et al. (2016) challenge the increasingly widespread use of Heckman models for endogeneity other than sample-induced endogeneity, and show that IV regressions are more appropriate in these cases. Therefore, we choose the IV-type regression to be our main regression framework.

Our first instrument is the share of equity crowdfunding financing rounds among those early-stage financing rounds in our extended (i.e. pre-matching) sample. These must stem from the respective country and industry and must have occurred within the 365 days prior to the focal funding round. Our second instrument is the natural logarithm of the USD amount of capital that companies in our extended (i.e. pre-matching) sample raised through equity crowdfunding rounds in the respective country and industry during the 365 days prior to the focal funding round. The use of two instruments allows us to test for instrument exogeneity (the fact that instruments are not correlated with the unobserved determinants of company performance), using the Hansen-J-statistic. However, note that the Hansen-J-test is unbiased and consistent only if at least one of the instruments is exogenous (Murray, 2006). We are convinced that this prerequisite is fulfilled. Both instruments are constructed at the macro-level and capture different aspects of equity crowdfunding proliferation. Hence, it would be highly puzzling if both instruments were correlated with performance outcomes at firm level (see Germann et al., 2015 for a similar argument).

In addition to instrument exogeneity, instrument relevance is the second important criterion for effective IV regressions (see Bascle, 2008 for an extensive discussion). We test the relevance of our instruments using the first-stage Kleibergen-Paap Wald rk F-statistic and compare it to the critical values of Stock and Yogo (2005). Since our instruments are slightly weak in most of the regressions, we use the Fuller (1977) modified limited information maximum likelihood (FULL) estimator, which is partially robust to weak instruments (e.g., Stock and Yogo, 2005) and preferable to limited information maximum likelihood estimates (LIML) (Bascle, 2008). The FULL estimate is thus a measure that can be used to address weak instruments (Bascle, 2008). Its statistics are robust to heteroscedasticity, but they are not efficient. Therefore, we additionally employ a continuously updated GMM estimator (CUE), which is a GMM-type LIML estimator (Hansen et al., 1996), and is recommended by Stock et al. (2002) in circumstances where heteroscedasticity is used as a second methodology. As an additional robustness check, we report the Moreira (2003) conditional likelihood ratio (CLR), since it is robust to finite-sample bias from arbitrarily weak instruments (e.g., Andrews et al., 2006). However, the Moreira CLR is not fully robust to heteroscedasticity (Moreira, 2003; Finlay and Magnusson, 2009).

Given that we use three different IV regression estimators (FULL, CUE, CLR) for those regressions in which endogeneity is present, it is important to stress that there exists no 'Swiss army knife' kind of regression that could overcome all obstacles at hand. Thus, it is important to assess the robustness of the findings across the different methods when interpreting our results (see Bertoni et al., 2011 for similar reasoning).

3.4 Empirical Results

In this section, we first present our sample and some univariate tests, then we discuss our results from OLS regressions, and then turn to more advanced tests of endogeneity and corresponding IV regressions.

3.4.1 Sample Overview and Univariate Tests

Our main sample consists of 7,396 company observations, of which 588 have completed an equity crowdfunding financing round. Tables 1 and 2 provide summary statistics for our sample by industry and year. It is not surprising that most of the recently founded ventures come from the services sector, according to the SIC classification (see Table 1). The main driver behind this finding is that software, app programming, and internet services are classified as a service in SIC terms. Mature, capital-intensive, and less innovative industries such as agriculture, mining, and public administration play only a minor role in the start-up landscape and are thus sparsely represented in the sample.

Table 1: Sample distribution by industry

SIC Division	Number of companies	Share
Agriculture, Forestry and Fishing	11	0.1%
Mining	4	0.1%
Manufacturing	313	4.2%
Transportation, Communications, Electric, Gas and Sanitary Service	350	4.7%
Retail Trade	751	10.2%
Finance, Insurance and Real Estate	722	9.8%
Services	5,237	70.8%
Public Administration	8	0.1%
Total	**7,396**	**100.0%**

Our sample overview by country (Table 2) shows that the majority of companies in our sample are based in the US. This finding is consistent with the fact that the US has the largest start-up and VC market globally. That being said, equity crowdfunding in the US had been strictly regulated and was accessible only to accredited investors (i.e., wealthy individuals) (Agrawal et al., 2014) prior to the deregulation pursuant to the JOBS Act in 2016 (Pisani, 2016). Hence, a high weighting of US companies in the sample could be problematic for the generalizability of our findings.[9] Therefore, we run an additional robustness check in Section 3.7.4 in which we assess the findings for a subsample of companies from countries with a more developed and less regulated equity crowdfunding market.

The distribution of the sample by founding year and funding year (Table 3) shows that the importance of equity crowdfunding is growing. There is an increasing number of equity crowdfunding rounds and the amounts raised are notable. While only 44 of the companies founded in 2010 used equity crowdfunding, almost five times as many companies founded in 2014 took advantage of it. Moreover, the companies in our sample raised USD 412 million capital through equity crowdfunding, a sizeable amount compared to the capital amounts raised by peers (USD 5,621 million).

---

9 We thank an anonymous referee for emphasizing this potential shortcoming.

Table 2: Sample distribution by country

Country	Peers		ECF	
	# of companies	Share	# of companies	Share
Australia	13	0.2%	2	0.3%
Belgium	3	0.0%	1	0.2%
Brasil	13	0.2%	2	0.3%
Canada	164	2.4%	27	4.6%
Finland	1	0.0%	1	0.2%
France	19	0.3%	3	0.5%
Germany	45	0.7%	7	1.2%
Great Britain	757	11.1%	183	31.1%
Hong-Kong	7	0.1%	1	0.2%
India	3	0.0%	1	0.2%
Ireland	9	0.1%	2	0.3%
Israel	3	0.0%	2	0.3%
Italy	2	0.0%	1	0.2%
Mexico	6	0.1%	1	0.2%
Netherlands	27	0.4%	6	1.0%
Nigeria	2	0.0%	1	0.2%
Romania	2	0.0%	1	0.2%
Spain	59	0.9%	12	2.0%
Sweden	5	0.1%	1	0.2%
Switzerland	4	0.1%	1	0.2%
United States	5,664	83.2%	332	56.5%
Total	**6,808**	**100.0%**	**588**	**100.0%**

Before we begin our main analyses, we compare equity-crowdfunded companies and peers using several univariate t-tests of overarching performance indicators (Table 4). While inferences from these analyses are limited due to their univariate nature, the results indicate that equity-crowdfunded companies seem to underperform compare to their peers. On average, they collect significantly less funding, raise fewer funding rounds over their lifetimes, have fewer employees and go public less frequently. In the next section, we explore these findings in more detail using multivariate analyses.

Table 3: Sample distribution by founding year and funding year

Year	Number of company foundations		Number of focal funding rounds		Raised amount in mUSD	
	Peers	ECF	Peers	ECF	Peers	ECF
2010	503	44	234	1	137.9	0.4
2011	898	58	13	1	5.4	0.0
2012	1,607	122	527	12	352.1	3.0
2013	1,964	161	1,719	59	1,235.1	21.1
2014	1,836	203	2,386	309	1,843.0	145.1
2015	-	-	1,449	144	1,479.5	154.1
2016	-	-	480	62	567.9	87.9
Total	**6,808**	**588**	**6,808**	**588**	**5,620.8**	**411.7**

Table 3 shows an overview of our sample clustered by founding year and funding year of the focal (i.e. treatment) funding round. The treatment funding round is defined as the first equity crowdfunding round for equity-crowdfunded (ECF) companies and as the matched funding round for peers. For more details on the matching procedure, please refer to Section 3.3.4. The amount raised in mUSD is the sum of funds collected in the treatment rounds of the companies in our sample in the respective year.

Table 4: Univariate comparison of equity-crowdfunded companies and peers

Variable	Peer companies		ECF companies		Mean difference
	Mean	SD	Mean	SD	t-value
Funding total (mUSD)	3.86	15.81	1.79	8.38	3.14***
Number of funding rounds	1.95	1.28	1.57	1.25	7.05***
IPO/Acquistion dummy	0.04	0.21	0.01	0.08	4.42***
Number of employees	30.7	166.7	17.7	49.4	1.88*

Table 4 shows an overview of our sample in the context of four variables. The funding total is the total amount of funding in mUSD that the companies in our sample have collected between their foundation and the reference date of our analyses. The number of funding rounds is the total number of funding rounds the companies have raised over their lifetimes. The *IPO/Acquisition dummy* is equal to 1 if a company went public or had been acquired prior to our reference date, and 0 otherwise. Number of employees is as of our reference date.

3.4.2 OLS Results and Tests for Endogeneity

First, our OLS regressions on interim success show that equity-crowdfunded companies are less likely to raise at least one follow-on funding round and also tend to raise fewer follow-on rounds and less capital generally (Table 5, Columns 1–3). These findings are significant at the 1% level. Taken together, these results provide evidence supporting the view that equity-crowdfunded companies achieve less interim success than their peers. The same holds true for terminal success. The coefficient for the *ECF dummy* is negative and significant at the 1% level in the regression of *IPO/Acquisition* as a dependent variable (Table 5, Column 4). The lesser success of equity-crowdfunded companies also manifests in operating performance (Table 5, Columns 5–6), as these companies are significantly smaller in terms of employees, which suggests slower growth, given that we employ a very strict matching procedure on company age. Moreover, they also show slower growth in terms of their social media footprint.

These findings are not only statistically significant but are also significant economically. For instance, the difference between equity-crowdfunded start-ups and peers in terms of the number of follow-on rounds is -0.27 (Table 5, Column 2), and the (untabulated) predicted outcomes are 0.58 for peers and 0.31 for equity-crowdfunded companies. Put differently, peers raise, on average, 0.58 follow-on rounds while equity-crowdfunded companies raise only 0.31 – hence, the predicted number of follow-on rounds is 87% higher for peers than for equity-crowdfunded companies. Also, the coefficient for the *ECF dummy* in our regression of *ln(Employees)* suggests that equity-crowdfunded companies have 29.8% fewer employees than peers. Although our measure for employees might be too coarse to allow for such exact inferences, the magnitude of the effect certainly highlights that the differences between equity-crowdfunded companies and peers are economically meaningful. This is especially the case given that we employed a strict matching procedure. However, even though these initial findings suggest that equity-crowdfunded companies underperform significantly compared to their peers, it is too early to draw causal inferences about the value-added by investors, as we need to test for endogeneity explicitly.

To test for the endogenous relationship between the equity crowdfunding of a company and company performance, we estimate differences in Sargan-Hansen statistics for the *ECF dummy* in all our regressions. This approach is robust to heteroscedasticity and is, thus, appropriate for our case (Baum et al., 2003).

Table 5: OLS regressions of start-up performance indicators

Variable	(1) OLS At least 1 follow-on round	(2) OLS # follow-on rounds	(3) OLS ln(Follow on total amount)	(4) OLS Acquistion/ IPO	(5) OLS ln(Employ- ees)	(6) HECKMAN ln(Likes growth)
ECF dummy	-0.205***	-0.265***	-3.051***	-0.0193***	-0.298***	-0.0507***
	(-12.47)	(-7.308)	(-13.33)	(-4.364)	(-7.480)	(-2.717)
Age	-4.32e-05	-0.000113	-0.000415	6.17e-06	0.000266***	5.34e-05
	(-0.928)	(-1.216)	(-0.614)	(0.326)	(2.605)	(1.358)
Time since focal	2.95e-05	0.000114	0.000227	4.43e-05**	-0.000389***	-0.000142***
funding round	(0.561)	(1.008)	(0.299)	(1.980)	(-3.261)	(-3.199)
Lambda						-0.217
						(-1.008)
Constant	0.783***	1.361**	11.67***	-0.0590	3.013***	0.355
	(3.131)	(2.529)	(3.202)	(-0.737)	(5.831)	(1.402)
Industry FE	YES	YES	YES	YES	YES	YES
Country FE	YES	YES	YES	YES	YES	YES
Founding year FE	YES	YES	YES	YES	YES	YES
Focal funding round year FE	YES	YES	YES	YES	YES	YES
R-squared	0.060	0.073	0.063	0.025	0.036	-
Adjusted R-squared	0.0517	0.0683	0.0579	0.0192	0.0306	-
N	7,396	7,396	7,396	7,396	7,396	7,396

Table 5 shows OLS regressions of the start-up performance indicators for our baseline sample. Regressions 1–6 are standard OLS regressions with robust standard errors. Regression 7 includes Lambda, a Heckman (1979) correction term for unobservable heterogeneity based on a first stage-regression, since the dependent variable is only available for a subset of companies. The *ECF dummy* is equal to 1 if a company has raised an equity crowdfunding investment round and 0 otherwise. *At least 1 follow-on round* is a dummy variable that is equal to 1 if companies have raised at least one subsequent financing round between their focal funding round and our reference date. *# follow-on rounds* reflects the number of follow-on financing rounds. *Ln(Follow on total amount)* is the natural logarithm of the amount of capital raised in subsequent rounds. *IPO/Acquisition* is a dummy variable that is equal to 1 if a company went public or had been acquired prior to our reference date and 0 otherwise. *Ln(Employees)* is the natural logarithm of the number of employees that companies have at our reference date. *Ln(Likes growth)* is the natural logarithm of growth in the number of 'Facebook likes' between March 2017 and July 2017. Definitions of the remaining variables are presented in Section 3.3.3. Robust t-statistics are reported in parentheses. *, **, and *** denote statistical significance at the 10%, 5%, and 1% levels, respectively.

Table 6: Endogeneity Test of the ECF dummy

Variable	(1) At least 1 follow-on round	(2) # follow-on rounds	(3) ln(Follow on total amount)	(4) Acquis-tion/ IPO	(5) ln(Em-ploy-ees)	(6) ln(Likes growth)
Test statistic	4.347	7.16	4.335	4.755	0.283	0.381
P-value	0.0371**	0.0075***	0.0373**	0.0292**	0.5945	0.5369

Table 6 shows differences in Sargan-Hansen statistics and accompanying p-values for our key variable *ECF dummy* in the regressions. *, **, and *** denote statistical significance at the 10%, 5%, and 1% levels, respectively

Table 6 details our findings for the different performance variables. Overall, we find endogeneity, indicated by significant p-values, in four of the regressions, including our analyses on ultimate success as well as all aspects of follow-on funding. First and foremost, these findings suggest that there is indeed an endogenous relationship between companies' choice of funding source and their performance in terms of these four dimensions, which is a very interesting additional finding. In the following section, we reassess these regressions with methods that are robust to endogeneity and are, thus, suited for making causal inferences. However, we do not find evidence of endogeneity in the regressions of the operating performance based on differences in Sargan-Hansen statistics. It is therefore plausible that the results from the OLS regressions and the Heckman correction are causally driven by the equity crowdfunding round. Moreover, the differences among the performance metrics underpin the advantages of the use of multiple measures for company success.

3.4.3 Analyses Accounting for Endogeneity of Financing Choice

When accounting for the endogeneity of financing choice and performance by using IV techniques (namely CUE, FULL, CLR – see Section 3.3.5 for details) in the four regressions for which indications for endogeneity can be found, we find that the results from the OLS regressions change partially. The coefficient of the *ECF dummy* in the regression of *IPO/Acquisition* (Table 7, Columns 4 and 8) shows the greatest change relative to the OLS results – it is no longer negative and significant at the 1% level, but is, instead, far from significant (t-statistic of 0.48 in Column 4). The strong underperformance of equity-crowdfunded companies we measure in the OLS regression no longer persists after we account for endogeneity. In other words, the lower rate of an IPO or acquisition of equity-crowdfunded companies is caused by the self-selection of low-quality companies into this funding type, as opposed to a negative effect (i.e. a disadvantage) from lower investor value-added following the equity crowdfunding round.

Nonetheless, the results for the follow-on funding parameters persist in the IV regressions (Table 7, Columns 1–3 and 5–7), although the coefficients are slightly smaller. For instance, the significance of the *ECF dummy* coefficient in the regressions of the number of follow-on rounds changes from 1% to 5% relative to the OLS. However, the results from the FULL and CUE regressions are very consistent, and both the significance as well as the magnitude of the coefficient for the *ECF dummy* are very similar (e.g., when comparing Columns 1 and 5 of Table 7), which indicates that the findings regarding follow-on funding are robust to methods that account for the potential endogeneity of the financing choice. However, the instruments are slightly weak in the FULL regression, where the first-stage Kleibergen-Paap F-statistic of 10.52 falls slightly below the critical value of 10.89 for a 10% Fuller maximum relative bias, according to Stock and Yogo (2002). Although the first-stage F-statistic in the CUE regression is above the critical value of 8.68 (maximum LIML size), we should compare the findings to those of the Moreira (2003) CLR analysis, to rule out that weak instruments led to biased coefficients in our analyses (the CLR analysis is robust to arbitrarily weak instruments – see Section 3.4. for details).

Table 8 shows that the results of the Moreira CLR analysis are in line with the FULL and CUE regressions. All coefficients that were significant in the FULL and CUE regressions remain negative and significant, even at the 1% level, as indicated by the coverage-corrected confidence intervals (see the third last row in Table 8) and the p-values, which are consistently below 0.01 (see the penultimate row in Table 8). Hence, we can conclude that the IV findings are consistent and that they are not affected by finite-sample bias. This is especially so given the fact that our instruments are exogenous, as indicated by the Hansen J-statistics. These results indicate that raising funds via an equity crowdfunding round has a causal negative effect on the success of subsequent funding attempts by a company when compared with raising funds via an investment round using traditional investors. Hence, we can conclude that equity crowdfunding investors add less value than traditional investors in terms of securing follow-on financing for early-stage ventures. We discuss the potential reasons for and implications of this result in the next section, but first, we run additional analyses to answer questions that have arisen from our findings hitherto.

3.4.4 Additional Analyses and Robustness Checks

To assess the degree to which our findings can be generalised, we run two major robustness checks that contemplate the regulatory environment within which equity crowdfunding is occurring. Across the countries in our sample, there are different regulatory frameworks that affect the attractiveness of crowdfunding relative to seed or angel financing. For instance, the regulations regarding the maximum amount of capital that start-ups can raise through equity crowdfunding differs depending on the location of the start-up. Moreover, in certain jurisdictions, the availability of crowdfunding to individual funders is contingent on particular characteristics, such as net worth and income (e.g., Hornuf and Schwienbacher, 2014). Hence, regulation could be an important *enabler* that assists an equity crowdfunding ecosystem to function (Davidsson et al., 2018).

First, although our research design explicitly addresses endogeneity through IV regressions and a strict matching procedure, we want to rule out the possibility that our findings on company performance and investor value-added could be partially driven by particularly successful peers that have raised funding amounts exceeding the regulatory limits for equity crowdfunding. To address this concern, we construct a subsample that excludes all peers who raised funds exceeding the maximum funding amount permitted with equity crowdfunding in the focal country. Consequently, our sample of equity-crowdfunded companies needs to be reduced, as there are in some cases no peers available when using this stricter matching paradigm. The subsample therefore includes 535 equity-crowdfunded companies and 5,284 peers.

Table 7: Instrumental variable (FULL and CUE) regressions for selected performance indicators

Variable	(1) FULL At least 1 follow-on round	(2) FULL # follow-on rounds	(3) FULL ln(Follow on total amount)	(4) FULL Acquisition/ IPO	(5) CUE At least 1 follow-on round	(6) CUE # follow-on rounds	(7) CUE ln(Follow on total amount)	(8) CUE Acquis- tion/ IPO
ECF dummy	-0.774***	-1.577**	-11.21***	0.0495	-0.770***	-1.674**	-10.99***	0.126
	(-2.681)	(-2.319)	(-2.695)	(0.483)	(-2.692)	(-2.440)	(-2.685)	(1.529)
Age	-0.000125**	-0.000303**	-0.00159*	1.61e-05	-0.000126**	-0.000315**	-0.00158*	2.79e-05
	(-1.969)	(-2.137)	(-1.729)	(0.688)	(-1.981)	(-2.187)	(-1.722)	(1.294)
Time since focal funding round	-3.60e-05	-3.74e-05	-0.000712	5.22e-05*	-3.31e-05	-5.61e-05	-0.000645	6.61e-05***
	(-0.568)	(-0.264)	(-0.772)	(1.877)	(-0.524)	(-0.406)	(-0.706)	(2.608)
Constant	0.711***	1.091**	9.484***	-0.0743	0.715***	1.173**	9.428***	-0.122**
	(3.465)	(2.485)	(3.223)	(-1.143)	(3.447)	(2.572)	(3.188)	(-2.100)
Industry FE	YES	YES	YES	YES	YES	YES	YES	YES
Country FE	YES	YES	YES	YES	YES	YES	YES	YES
Founding year FE	YES	YES	YES	YES	YES	YES	YES	YES
Focal funding round year FE	YES	YES	YES	YES	YES	YES	YES	YES
Kleibergen-Paap rk LM	19.69	19.69	19.69	19.69	19.69	19.69	19.69	19.69
Kleibergen-Paap rk LM p-value	0.000	0.000	0.000	0.000	0.000	0.000	0.000	0.000
Kleibergen-Paap rk F-statistic (rk Wald)	10.52	10.52	10.52	10.52	10.52	10.52	10.52	10.52

Variable	(1) FULL At least 1 follow-on round	(2) FULL # follow-on rounds	(3) FULL ln(Follow on total amount)	(4) FULL Acquisition/ IPO	(5) CUE At least 1 follow-on round	(6) CUE # follow-on rounds	(7) CUE ln(Follow on total amount)	(8) CUE Acquisition/ IPO
Critical value 10% Fuller max. rel. bias	10.89	10.89	10.89	10.89	n.m.	n.m.	n.m.	n.m.
Critical value 10% maximal LIML size	n.m.	n.m.	n.m.	n.m.	8.68	8.68	8.68	8.68
Hansen J-statistic	1.114	0.134	1.012	1.267	1.126	0.132	1.025	1.223
Hansen J-statistic p-value	0.291	0.714	0.315	0.260	0.289	0.716	0.311	0.269
N	7,396	7,396	7,396	7,396	7,396	7,396	7,396	7,396

Table 7 shows Instrumental variable regressions for those analyses for which endogeneity was found (see Table 6). Regressions 1–4 use the FULL estimator and Regressions 5–8 employ a CUE. Respective critical values stem from Stock and Yogo (2002). The *ECF dummy* is equal to 1 if a firm has raised an equity crowdfunding investment round and 0 otherwise. *At least 1 follow-on round* is a dummy variable that is equal to 1 if firms have raised at least one subsequent financing round between their focal funding round and our reference date. *# follow-on rounds* reflects the number of follow-on financing rounds. *Ln(Follow on total amount)* is the natural logarithm of the amount of capital raised in subsequent rounds. *IPO/Acquisition* is a dummy variable that is equal to 1 if a firm went public or had been acquired prior to our reference date and 0 otherwise. Definitions of the remaining variables are presented in Section 3.3.3. Robust *z*-statistics are reported in parentheses. *, **, and *** denote statistical significance at the 10%, 5% and 1% levels, respectively.

Table 8: CLR confidence intervals for coefficients of ECF dummy in regressions of selected performance indicators

Variable	(1) CLR At least 1 follow-on round	(2) CLR # follow-on rounds	(3) CLR ln(Follow on total amount)	(4) CLR Acquistion/IPO
ECF dummy	-0.790**	-1.613**	-11.44**	0.0515
	(-2.531)	(-2.510)	(-2.528)	(0.400)
Age	-0.000128*	-0.000308**	-0.00163*	1.64e-05
	(-1.919)	(-2.235)	(-1.687)	(0.600)
Time since focal funding round	-3.79e-05	-4.15e-05	-0.000738	5.25e-05*
	(-0.578)	(-0.305)	(-0.776)	(1.949)
Constant	1.452**	4.009***	20.85**	-0.215
	(2.544)	(3.385)	(2.519)	(-0.918)
Industry FE	YES	YES	YES	YES
Country FE	YES	YES	YES	YES
Founding year FE	YES	YES	YES	YES
Focal funding round year FE	YES	YES	YES	YES

Variable	(1) CLR At least 1 follow-on round	(2) CLR # follow-on rounds	(3) CLR ln(Follow on total amount)	(4) CLR Acquisition/IPO
95% coverage-corrected confidence set of coefficient on ECF dummy	[-1.525711, -0.199695]	[-3.138597, -0.4112963]	[-22.07246, -2.868584]	[-0.2119332, 0.3326839]
p-value	0.0092	0.0087	0.0094	0.693
N	7,396	7,396	7,396	7,396

Table 8 shows Instrumental variable regressions for those analyses for which endogeneity was found (see Table 6), as well as the corresponding Moreira (2003) CLR estimator in the form of a coverage-corrected confidence set of the coefficient from the IV regressions, as well as the p-value for Ho: _b[ECF_new] = 0. The ECF dummy is equal to 1 if a company has raised an equity crowdfunding investment round and 0 otherwise. At least 1 follow-on round is a dummy variable that is equal to 1 if companies have raised at least one subsequent financing round between their focal funding round and our reference date. # follow-on rounds reflects the number of follow-on financing rounds. Ln(Follow on total amount) is the natural logarithm of the amount of capital raised in subsequent rounds. IPO/Acquisition is a dummy variable that is equal to 1 if a company went public or had been acquired prior to our reference date and 0 otherwise. Definitions of the remaining variables are presented in Section 3.3.3. T-statistics are reported in parentheses. *, **, and *** denote statistical significance at the 10%, 5% and 1% levels, respectively.

Table 9: OLS regressions of performance indicators in subsample excluding peers raising high amounts of funding

Variable	(1) OLS At least 1 follow-on round	(2) OLS # follow-on rounds	(3) OLS ln(Follow on total amount)	(4) OLS Acquisition/IPO	(5) OLS ln(Employees)	(6) HECKMAN ln(Likes growth)
ECF dummy	-0.181***	-0.231***	-2.568***	-0.0187***	-0.225***	-0.0508**
	(-10.21)	(-5.742)	(-10.57)	(-4.795)	(-5.654)	(-2.388)
Age	-5.91e-05	-0.000101	-0.000740	1.02e-05	0.000202*	5.46e-05
	(-1.135)	(-0.937)	(-1.014)	(0.506)	(1.837)	(1.135)
Time since focal funding round	6.35e-05	0.000350***	0.000914	2.76e-05	-0.000187	-0.000117**
	(1.078)	(2.638)	(1.110)	(1.178)	(-1.485)	(-2.169)
Lambda						-0.0814
						(-0.365)
Constant	0.543**	0.421	8.148**	-0.0224	2.482***	0.190
	(2.278)	(0.737)	(2.407)	(-0.266)	(4.965)	(0.627)
Industry FE	YES	YES	YES	YES	YES	YES
Country FE	YES	YES	YES	YES	YES	YES
Founding year FE	YES	YES	YES	YES	YES	YES
Focal funding round year FE	YES	YES	YES	YES	YES	YES
R-squared	0.053	0.063	0.056	0.024	0.035	-
Adjusted R-squared	0.0466	0.0562	0.0492	0.0178	0.0285	-
N	5,819	5,819	5,819	5,819	5,819	5,819

Table 9 shows OLS regressions of start-up performance indicators for a subsample of companies that excludes peers which raised amounts of funding exceeding the respective regulatory threshold. Regressions 1–6 are standard OLS regressions with robust standard errors. Regression 7 includes Lambda, a Heckman (1979) correction term for unobservable heterogeneity based on a first stage-regression, since the dependent variable is only available for a subset of companies. The ECF dummy is equal to 1 if a company has raised an equity crowdfunding investment round and 0 otherwise. At least 1 follow-on round is a dummy variable that is equal to 1 if companies have raised at least one subsequent financing round between their focal funding round and our reference date. # follow-on rounds reflects the number of follow-on financing rounds. Ln(Follow on total amount) is the natural logarithm of the amount of capital raised in subsequent rounds. IPO/Acquisition is a dummy variable that is equal to 1 if a company went public or had been acquired prior to our reference date and 0 otherwise. Ln(Employees) is the natural logarithm of the number of employees that companies have at our reference date. Ln(Likes growth) is the natural logarithm of the growth in the number of 'Facebook likes' between March 2017 and July 2017. Definitions of the remaining variables are presented in Section 3.3.3. Robust t-statistics are reported in parentheses. *, ** and *** denote statistical significance at the 10%, 5% and 1% levels, respectively.

Table 10: *Endogeneity test of the ECF dummy in subsample excluding peers raising high amounts of funding*

Variable	(1) At least 1 follow-on round	(2) # follow-on rounds	(3) ln(Follow on total amount)	(4) Acquisition/IPO	(5) ln(Employees)	(6) ln(Likes growth)
Test statistic	4.287	3.68	4.113	6.752	0.008	0.459
P-value	0.0384**	0.0551*	0.0426**	0.0094***	0.9284	0.4981

Table 10 shows differences in Sargan-Hansen statistics and accompanying p-values for our key variable *ECF dummy* in the different regressions. *, ** and *** denote statistical significance at the 10%, 5% and 1% levels, respectively.

Our first step is to turn to the OLS results of this subsample analysis shown in Table 9. Compared to the OLS results from our main sample, shown in Table 5, the significance of the results is extremely robust – all coefficients for the *ECF dummy* remain negative and significant at a rate of 1% or 5%. However, the magnitude of the *ECF dummy* coefficient decreases in all regressions, which is plausible given that we exclude peers who structurally raised greater amounts of capital in the focal funding round (and, thus, presumably have better prospects for high growth and performance in the post-funding period).

When we assess the endogeneity of company financing choice and performance (Table 10), we also find results that are very consistent with those from our main sample. In four of the six regressions (Table 10, Columns 1–4), we find significant evidence for endogeneity according to the Sargan-Hansen statistics. Further, the IV regressions for the subsample are very consistent with the results from the main sample (Tables 11 and 12).

As expected from the OLS regressions, we find smaller coefficients and slightly lower levels of significance but, as before, the results point to a causal negative treatment effect with regard to the follow-on funding performance of equity-crowdfunded companies (Table 11, Columns 1–3 and 5–8 and Table 12, Columns 1–3). Moreover, the coefficients in the regressions for the amount of *At least 1 follow-on round* and *ln(Follow on total amount)* remain negative and significant at the 5% level, while the coefficient related to the regressions of the number of follow-on rounds is significant at the 10% level. Again, we find no negative causal influence on the propensity of an IPO or acquisition (Tables 11 and 12, Column 4, respectively).[10]

Therefore, we can conclude that even where we perform a comparison of equity-crowdfunded companies and peers with very similar valuation and capital requirements, we still find a pattern of adverse selection (i.e. endogeneity) and we still find a negative causal treatment effect of the equity crowdfunding round on post-funding performance. This provides evi-

---

10 In the regressions of *IPO/Acquisition*, the coefficient of the *ECF dummy* turns positive and becomes weakly significant at the 10% level (t-statistic of 1.71) in the CUE regression (Table 11, Column 8). However, this finding is not robust across the different IV regressions and is economically implausible, given the overall findings using the other analyses and methods. We therefore believe that this is instead an artefact which manifests the very strong selection effect, driving the OLS results to be negative and significant at the 1% level.

dence of an inferior value-added provided by equity crowdfunding investors.

Second, we want to assess if the economics of equity crowdfunding might be different in countries where regulation is more liberal and where it constitutes a more established funding alternative. While these conditions would, according to our assessment, primarily affect the adverse selection pattern, it could also be possible that investors provide greater value-added in these countries, too. Hence, we examine whether the two findings – inferior investor value-added and endogeneity – also exist in those countries with more liberal crowdfunding regulations. To do this, we construct a subsample that excludes all companies in countries with rigid rules regarding crowdfunding. In particular, we exclude companies from the US, since equity crowdfunding was deregulated only when the JOBS Act became effective in May 2016 (Hornuf and Schwienbacher, 2014).

We further exclude German companies, since common equity shares can be issued up to an amount of only EUR 100,000 in Germany without the filing of a full prospectus, and larger amounts can only be raised via participatory loans (Klöhn et al., 2015). Therefore, participatory loans are the dominant form of crowdfunding in Germany, but they are not suited to early-stage, high-risk ventures without substantial cash flow. This is because these companies are not able to pay interest and, thus, participatory loans are not a fully viable alternative to angel and VC financing.[11] Moreover, we exclude all companies from countries in which no significant equity crowdfunding financing (raised amount exceeding USD 50,000) has taken place.[12]

---

11 Our findings are robust to keeping the German observations though.
12 The findings are also robust when using USD 100,000 as a threshold.

Table 11: *Instrumental variable (FULL and CUE) regressions of selected performance indicators in subsample excluding peers raising high amounts of funding*

Variable	(1) FULL	(2) FULL	(3) FULL	(4) FULL	(5) CUE	(6) CUE	(7) CUE	(8) CUE
	At least 1 follow-on round	# follow-on rounds	ln(Follow on total amount)	Acquistion/IPO	At least 1 follow-on round	# follow-on rounds	ln(Follow on total amount)	Acquistion/IPO
ECF dummy	-0.799**	-1.387*	-11.01**	0.138	-0.813**	-1.487*	-11.13**	0.173*
	(-2.390)	(-1.817)	(-2.359)	(1.147)	(-2.362)	(-1.901)	(-2.322)	(1.706)
Age	-0.000147**	-0.000265*	-0.00194*	3.23e-05	-0.000150**	-0.000277*	-0.00197*	3.74e-05
	(-2.032)	(-1.674)	(-1.917)	(1.239)	(-2.038)	(-1.713)	(-1.918)	(1.516)
Time since focal funding round	-3.04e-05	0.000174	-0.000370	5.14e-05	-3.14e-05	0.000153	-0.000366	5.84e-05*
	(-0.383)	(0.968)	(-0.332)	(1.527)	(-0.391)	(0.864)	(-0.325)	(1.910)
Constant	0.728***	0.883*	9.111***	-0.115	0.734***	0.939*	9.160***	-0.135*
	(3.055)	(1.843)	(2.840)	(-1.463)	(3.027)	(1.905)	(2.805)	(-1.857)
Industry FE	YES	YES	YES	YES	YES	YES	YES	YES
Country FE	YES	YES	YES	YES	YES	YES	YES	YES
Founding year FE	YES	YES	YES	YES	YES	YES	YES	YES
Focal funding round year FE	YES	YES	YES	YES	YES	YES	YES	YES
Kleibergen-Paap rk LM	14.53	14.53	14.53	14.53	14.53	14.53	14.53	14.53
Kleibergen-Paap rk LM p-value	0.000701	0.000701	0.000701	0.000701	0.000701	0.000701	0.000701	0.000701

Variable	(1) FULL At least 1 follow-on round	(2) FULL # follow-on rounds	(3) FULL ln(Follow on total amount)	(4) FULL Acquisition/IPO	(5) CUE At least 1 follow-on round	(6) CUE # follow-on rounds	(7) CUE ln(Follow on total amount)	(8) CUE Acquisition/IPO
Kleibergen-Paap F-statistic (rk Wald)	7.474	7.474	7.474	7.474	7.474	7.474	7.474	7.474
Critical value 10% Fuller max. rel. bias	10.89	10.89	10.89	10.89	n.m.	n.m.	n.m.	n.m.
Critical value 10% maximal LIML size	n.m.	n.m.	n.m.	n.m.	8.68	8.68	8.68	8.68
Hansen J-statistic	0.385	0.0755	0.328	0.146	0.383	0.0745	0.328	0.142
Hansen J-statistic p-value	0.535	0.783	0.567	0.703	0.536	0.785	0.567	0.707
N	5,819	5,819	5,819	5,819	5,819	5,819	5,819	5,819

Table 11 shows Instrumental variable regressions for those analyses for which endogeneity was found (see Table 10) in a subsample of companies that excludes peers which raised amounts of funding exceeding the respective regulatory threshold. Regressions 1–4 use the FULL estimator and Regressions 5–8 use the FULL (CUE) estimator. Respective critical values stem from Stock and Yogo (2002). The ECF dummy is equal to 1 if a company has raised an equity crowdfunding investment round and 0 otherwise. At least 1 follow-on round is a dummy variable that is equal to 1 if companies have raised at least one subsequent financing round between their focal funding round and our reference date. # follow-on rounds reflects the number of follow-on financing rounds. Ln(Follow on total amount) is the natural logarithm of the amount of capital raised in subsequent rounds. IPO/Acquisition is a dummy variable that is equal to 1 if a company went public or had been acquired prior to our reference date and 0 otherwise. Definitions of the remaining variables are presented in Section 3.3.3. Robust z-statistics are reported in parentheses. *, ** and *** denote statistical significance at the 10%, 5% and 1% levels, respectively.

Table 12: CLR confidence intervals for coefficients of ECF dummy in regressions of selected performance indicators in subsample excluding peers raising high amounts of funding

Variable	(1) CLR At least 1 follow-on round	(2) CLR # follow-on rounds	(3) CLR ln(Follow on total amount)	(4) CLR Acquistion/IPO
ECF dummy	-0.825**	-1.436*	-11.37**	0.144
	(-2.250)	(-1.857)	(-2.219)	(1.011)
Age	-0.000150**	-0.000272*	-0.00199*	3.33e-05
	(-1.969)	(-1.683)	(-1.861)	(1.116)
Time since focal funding round	-3.44e-05	0.000167	-0.000425	5.24e-05
	(-0.411)	(0.944)	(-0.363)	(1.607)
Constant	0.743**	0.911	9.314**	-0.119
	(2.503)	(1.452)	(2.245)	(-1.027)
Industry FE	YES	YES	YES	YES
Country FE	YES	YES	YES	YES
Founding year FE	YES	YES	YES	YES
Focal funding round year FE	YES	YES	YES	YES

Variable	(1) CLR At least 1 follow-on round	(2) CLR # follow-on rounds	(3) CLR ln(Follow on total amount)	(4) CLR Acquisition/IPO
95% coverage-corrected confidence set of coefficient on ECF dummy	[-1.775906, -0.138319]	[-3.401949, 0.0400108]	[-24.61352, -1.73875]	[-.1390874, 0.4941005]
p-value	0.0193	0.0563	0.0215	0.3105
N	5,819	5,819	5,819	5,819

Table 12 shows Instrumental variable regressions analyses for which endogeneity was found (see Table 10) in a subsample of companies that excludes peers which raised amounts of funding exceeding the respective regulatory threshold. Most importantly, it displays the corresponding Moreira (2003) CLR estimator in the form of a coverage-corrected confidence set of the coefficient from the IV regressions, as well as the p-value for Ho: _b[ECF_new] = 0. The ECF dummy is equal to 1 if a company has raised an equity crowdfunding investment round and 0 otherwise. At least 1 follow-on round is a dummy variable that is equal to 1 if companies have raised at least one subsequent financing round between their focal funding round and our reference date. # follow-on rounds reflects the number of follow-on financing rounds accordingly. Ln(Follow on total amount) is the natural logarithm of the amount of capital raised in subsequent rounds. IPO/Acquisition is a dummy variable that is equal to 1 if a company went public or had been acquired prior to our reference date and 0 otherwise. Ln(Employees) is the number of employees that companies have at our reference date. The definition of the remaining variables is presented in Section 3.3.3. T-statistics are reported in parentheses. *, **, and *** denote statistical significance at the 10%, 5% and 1% level, respectively

Table 13: OLS regressions of start-up performance indicators for subsample of companies from countries with more established equity crowdfunding systems

Variable	(1) OLS At least 1 follow-on round	(2) OLS # follow-on rounds	(3) OLS ln(Follow on total amount)	(4) OLS Acquistion/IPO	(5) OLS ln(Employees)	(6) HECKMAN ln(Likes growth)
ECF dummy	-0.0581*	0.0558	-0.864**	-0.0194***	-0.143**	-0.0378
	(-1.888)	(0.713)	(-2.029)	(-2.780)	(-2.103)	(-0.528)
Age	-9.05e-05	-0.000489**	-0.00130	1.85e-05	7.06e-05	0.000132
	(-0.856)	(-2.196)	(-0.878)	(0.599)	(0.321)	(0.568)
Time since focal funding round	0.000462***	0.00103***	0.00619***	3.50e-06	-0.000428*	-6.44e-05
	(3.831)	(4.110)	(3.694)	(0.0822)	(-1.750)	(-0.247)
Lambda						-5.473
						(-0.243)
Constant	-0.127	-0.103	-0.813	-0.104	3.698***	2.717
	(-0.307)	(-0.125)	(-0.141)	(-0.775)	(4.200)	(0.211)
Industry FE	YES	YES	YES	YES	YES	YES
Country FE	YES	YES	YES	YES	YES	YES
Founding year FE	YES	YES	YES	YES	YES	YES
Focal funding round year FE	YES	YES	YES	YES	YES	YES
R-squared	0.096	0.122	0.102	0.022	0.072	-
Adjusted R-squared	0.0756	0.102	0.0815	-0.000650	0.0506	-
N	1,332	1,332	1,332	1,332	1,332	1,332

Table 13 shows OLS regressions of start-up performance indicators for a subsample of companies from countries with liberal equity crowdfunding regulation and a more established equity crowdfunding system. Regressions 1–6 are standard OLS regressions with robust standard errors. Regression 7 includes *Lambda*, a Heckman (1979) correction term for unobservable heterogeneity based on a first stage-regression, since the dependent variable is only available for a subset of companies. The *ECF dummy* is equal to 1 if a company has raised an equity crowdfunding investment round and 0 otherwise. *Ln(treatment amount)* is the natural logarithm of the amount of funds raised in the focal funding round. The focal funding round is defined as the first equity crowdfunding round for equity-crowdfunded companies and as the matching funding round for peers. For more details on the matching procedure, please refer to Section 3.3. *At least 1 follow-on round* is a dummy variable that is equal to 1 if companies have raised at least one subsequent financing round between their focal funding round and our reference date. *# follow-on rounds* reflects the number of follow-on financing rounds. *Ln(Follow on total amount)* is the natural logarithm of the amount of capital raised in subsequent rounds. *IPO/Acquisition* is a dummy variable that is equal to 1 if a company went public or had been acquired prior to our reference date and 0 otherwise. *Ln(Employees)* is the natural logarithm of the number of employees that companies have at our reference date. *Ln(Likes growth)* is the natural logarithm of the growth in the number of 'Facebook likes' between March 2017 and July 2017. Definitions of the remaining variables are presented in Section 3.3.3. Robust t-statistics are reported in parentheses. *, ** and *** denote statistical significance at the 10%, 5% and 1% levels, respectively.

Table 14: Endogeneity Test of the ECF dummy in a subsample of companies from countries with more established equity crowd-funding systems

	(1)	(2)	(3)	(4)	(5)	(6)
Variable	At least 1 follow-on round	# follow-on rounds	ln(Follow on total amount)	Acquisition/ IPO	ln(Employees)	ln(Likes growth)
Test statistic	0.003	0.711	0.016	0.135	0.09	0.125
P-value	0.9593	0.3993	0.9001	0.7128	0.7639	0.7237

Table 14 shows differences in Sargan-Hansen statistics and accompanying p-values for our key variable *ECF dummy* in the regressions. *, ** and *** denote statistical significance at the 10%, 5% and 1% levels, respectively.

Results from our analyses using this subsample are shown in Tables 13 and 14. In the OLS regression (Table 13), we find that the results are slightly weaker when compared to the full sample but are still in line with our main findings. For instance, the coefficient of the *ECF dummy* remains negative and significant at the 1% level in our regression of *IPO/Acquisition*. Moreover, the results in the regressions for follow-on funding (Table 13, Columns 1–3) and operating performance (Table 13, Columns 5–6) weaken commensurately with lower significance levels and smaller coefficients. However, we do not find evidence of the endogeneity of the *ECF dummy* in these regressions (Table 14) according to the Sargan-Hansen statistics. This finding suggests that, in countries with more liberal regulation and a more well-established crowdfunding ecosystem, high-quality companies regard equity crowdfunding as a viable funding alternative, and thus no adverse selection seems to be present. However, the equity crowdfunders add less value to start-up companies than professional investors in these countries too.

Taken together, these additional tests thus demonstrate that our findings are robust to multiple alternative model specifications as well as to several sample construction procedures.

3.5 Discussion

Overall, our analyses provide strong and robust evidence suggesting that that equity crowdfunders add less value to their investments than professional investors. We find a negative treatment effect for equity crowdfunding (relative to seed and angel financing) across the dimensions of interim and operating performance and the effect is robust to alternative model specifications and sample construction procedures.

While our empirical setting does not allow us to disentangle *how* the different value-adding factors (i.e. monitoring, provision of managerial competencies, access to networks, and endorsement) contribute to the difference in value-added (Dutta and Folta, 2016), our research does deliver important insights as to the overall value-adding contributions of both equity crowdfunders and traditional investors.

First, our findings confirm that traditional investors add value to portfolio companies relative to a novel 'control group', namely equity-crowdfunded ventures. This evidence supports recent findings outlined in the literature stream about value-added by investors, wherein VC investors and business angels are reported to improve the performance of their portfolio companies beyond the provision of capital (e.g., Chemmanur et al., 2011; Bertoni et al., 2011; Croce et al., 2013; Kerr et al., 2014). Specifically, our findings underscore the notion that investor support is a valuable resource for portfolio companies when it is applied appropriately (e.g., Colombo and Grilli, 2010; Lungeanu and Zajac, 2016).

Moreover, the findings from our research highlight that effective governance and a model for collaboration is a prerequisite to the resources of investors becoming accessible to entrepreneurs. To date, even though crowd investors could offer both managerial support (Schwienbacher and Larralde, 2010) and social capital (Sorensen and Stuart, 2001; Hochberg et al., 2007; Werth and Boeert, 2013) from their extensive networks, these resources remain unexploited because the channels through which entrepreneurs could engage and manage the large number of potentially distant crowd investors are effectively absent. This is particularly deplorable because the access to the expansive networks of crowd investors include potential customers and partners and could become a competitive advantage for equity-crowdfunded companies vis-à-vis VC and BA-backed peers. Consequently, we advocate the view that entrepreneurs need to complement their crowdfunding-based financing approach with measures of open strategy and innovation (Matzler et al., 2014; Schlagwein and Bjørn-Andersen; 2014; Sailer et al., 2017; Tavakoli et al., 2017) to draw on the valuable resources their investors have to offer. This recommendation is also supported by the findings of Stanko and Henard (2017) in the context of product crowdfunding. They suggest that companies do indeed benefit from drawing more intensely from the expertise of their crowd investors because the open search depth (the intensity with which companies draw from external sources) of crowdfundees enhances product market performance.

Moreover, as an additional finding, our results show that a firm's choice of equity crowdfunding as a funding source and their subsequent performance are endogenously determined (when all countries are included in our sample). Additionally, our findings regarding the regressions on terminal success (*IPO/Acquisition*) indicate a particularly strong negative selection effect, suggesting that lower-quality companies self-select into equity crowdfunding. This explanation is consistent with the notion of equity crowdfunding as a second-class funding mechanism that is less attractive to companies than traditional VC and BA financing. While it would certainly be beneficial to understand entrepreneurs' motives for this decision, our results provide a first hint: start-ups seem to consider equity crowdfunding as a viable funding alternative in countries with more liberal regulation and a more established crowdfunding ecosystem. This is evidenced by the absence of an observed endogenous relationship between choice in funding and subsequent performance within this sample. Nonetheless, the causal negative treatment effect of equity crowdfunding persists, although it is slightly weaker.[13] Taken together, these findings indicate that entrepreneurs base their decisions about equity crowdfunding on observable 'hard' factors, like the maximum amount of capital they can theoretically raise, and less on unobservable 'soft' factors, such as differences in value-adding capabilities. In that regard, our findings highlight that regulation is an important enabler for novel funding mechanisms, including equity crowdfunding, and that it plays a triggering role for the adoption of these funding alternatives by high-profile entrepreneurs (Davidsson et al., 2018).

Our research contributes to several streams of literature. First, we add to the literature on value-added by investors (e.g., Croce et al., 2013; Kerr et al., 2013; Dutta and Folta, 2016). We also extend it to equity crowdfunding, an area which has previously been underexplored (Dushnitsky and Zunino, 2018). In doing so, we advance the literature stream which is dedicated to the causal value-adding effects of early-stage investors (e.g., Chemmanur et al., 2011; Croce et al., 2013). Our work joins recent contributions which are working towards creating a more refined understanding of the differences in value-adding contributions by the increasing number of investor types (e.g., Grilli and Murtinu, 2014; Dutta and Folta, 2016). Second, our findings add to the entrepreneurial finance literature on crowdfunding (e.g., Agrawal et al., 2014; Mollick, 2014; Ahlers et al., 2015; Bruton et al., 2015; Stanko and Henard, 2017) by providing the first in-depth comparative analysis of the outcomes of equity crowdfunding. This is required to understand how crowdfunding impacts companies' pathways (Stanko and Henard, 2017; Dushnitsky and Zunino, 2018). This area of crowdfunding research has previously been underexplored, especially with respect to equity crowdfunding (Dushnitsky and Zunino, 2018), as most prior works focus on the signalling of crowdfundees, success drivers of funding campaigns or investor decision-making (e.g., Ahlers et al., 2015; Colombo et al., 2015; Kuppuswamy and Bayus, 2017). Moreover, extant studies related to the consequences of equity crowdfunding, such as Sig-

---

13 The weaker treatment effect detected in countries with more liberal crowdfunding regulation can also be associated with the fact that the venture capital ecosystem in these countries is smaller and less competitive than in the US; therefore, professional investors may engage in value-adding activities less frequently and/or they may have fewer resources and, therefore, less impact if they do engage.

nori and Vismara (2018), do not allow for *causal* inferences relative to other funding alternatives. In this context, we also raise awareness of the management and governance challenges associated with equity crowdfunding and highlight the importance of regulation for the adoption of innovative funding mechanisms, like crowdfunding (Davidsson et al., 2018). Finally, we add to the literature on openness (e.g., Hautz et al., 2017; Stanko and Henard, 2017) by exposing the need to complement 'open' funding practices (such as equity crowdfunding) with commensurate open strategy and innovation practices.

Practically, it is imperative that investors, crowdfundee companies and investment platforms address the current monitoring and governance deficits in order to establish equity crowdfunding as a funding source which is viable in the long run. First, providers of equity crowdfunding platforms need to put stronger governance measures in place. They could, for example, send a representative of the crowd to the board of funded companies or they could stage the payout of funds based on milestones. Moreover, in order to facilitate the provision of managerial competencies and access to crowdfunding investors' networks in a structured manner, we propose that crowdfundee companies engage in open strategy and innovation practices (e.g., Tavakoli et al., 2017). Platform providers can support this effort by providing an open strategy toolkit that draws on the competences of crowd investors and best practices that can be shared with portfolio companies. When designing their open strategy practices, early-stage ventures need to pay attention to the effective use of resources and assess confidentiality risks, as these common challenges in open strategy practice (Sailer et al., 2017) are particularly relevant for young ventures. Moreover, companies need to account for the potential drawbacks of crowdfunding when deciding whether to use crowdfunding in the first place.

Other than becoming more actively involved and emulating the value-adding of traditional investors, another possible solution for platform providers would be to partner with selected VC firms and syndicate deals with them. For instance, VC firms could conduct due diligence, invest alongside the 'crowd', and then help to monitor the portfolio companies whilst providing access to network and managerial expertise for later-stage development. Moreover, they could also serve as a more reputable signal to third parties (see Agrawal et al., 2016 for a similar discussion and overview of syndication in equity crowdfunding).

Finally, regulators can moderate part of the adverse selection problem if they make equity crowdfunding more attractive, especially by allowing higher funding volumes for start-ups (Hornuf and Schwienbacher, 2016). However, in practice, providers of equity crowdfunding platforms have the strongest incentive to address both the observed adverse selection of low-quality companies and the inferior value-added by crowdfunders, as they might otherwise be running 'markets for lemons' which are likely to go out of business in the long run.

This research has several limitations that offer avenues for future research. First, while our analyses are based on an international sample which includes data from multiple crowdfunding platforms, and thus offers a high degree of generalisability, this generalisability inherently comes at the price of accuracy (Thorngate, 1976; Dushnitsky and Fitza, 2018). It would therefore be interesting to obtain a more refined empirical understanding of the differences in value-added exposed by us. For instance, it would be worthwhile exploring whether there is heterogeneity *within* the different investor types by accounting for additional investor and funding round characteristics. In the same vein, and as a general goal for the literature stream on value-added by investors, it would be desirable to further disentangle *how* investors add value, and what individual impact the different causal factors have. Moreover, it would be important to empirically test our proposition that open strategy practices are suited to overcoming the drawbacks of a more complex investor–company relationship in the context of equity crowdfunding. Besides that, it is possible that there is some degree of sample selection bias within the Crunchbase dataset with respect to equity crowdfunding rounds, although, as already discussed, the overall dataset has very broad coverage that is superior to other datasets (Kaminski et al., 2019). Thus, if there were sample selection bias, it would most likely affect equity crowdfunding rounds more strongly than seed or angel rounds. However, the database would typically be biased toward equity-crowdfunded companies that have had more successful equity crowdfunding rounds and which gathered more attention from the investor community. Hence, these companies are presumably of higher quality than the average equity crowdfunding firm; therefore, sample selection bias would affect the results in the opposite direction of our findings and would not lead to false-positive findings. Finally, as an additional avenue for future research, it would be worthwhile to further explore the returns earned by equity crowdfunders and compare them to those of traditional investors. While our results suggest that equity crowdfunders' investments tend to underperform compared to those of professional investors, exploration of whether equity crowdfunders realise positive risk-adjusted returns or not remains incomplete.

3.6 Conclusion

This essay evaluates the performance of 588 equity-crowdfunded companies and 6,808 matched peers to compare the value-added of investors in equity crowdfunding with that of those undertaking traditional early-stage financing. Our research is the first to empirically scrutinise equity crowdfunders' value-adding contributions and the influence of equity crowdfunding on companies' subsequent development. The results show that equity-crowdfunded companies consistently underperform compared to their peers due to both adverse selection of low-quality companies into equity crowdfunding and a negative causal treatment effect of equity crowdfunding, as equity crowdfunders add less value than traditional investors. We argue that the inferior value-added of equity crowdfunders is caused by a combination of suboptimal monitoring, a more complex investor–company relationship that currently fails to make the potentially valuable managerial and social capital resources (i.e. networks) of crowd investors accessible to entrepreneurs, as well as inferior investor reputation. The findings are robust to alternative model specifications and sample construction procedures.

Our research contributes to several streams of literature. First, we add to the literature on investor value-added (e.g., Croce et al., 2013; Kerr et al., 2014; Grilli and Murtinu, 2014; Dutta and Folta, 2016) by extending it to equity crowdfunders as a new investor type. Second, our findings contribute to the emerging entrepreneurial finance literature on crowdfunding (e.g., Agrawal et al., 2014; Mollick, 2014; Stanko and Henard, 2017; Signori and Vismara, 2018) with the first comparative analysis of the outcomes from equity crowdfunding – a critical step leading to better understanding of crowdfunding's influence on companies' subsequent development (Stanko and Henard, 2017; Dushnitsky and Zunino, 2018). Moreover, we also raise awareness about the management and governance challenges associated with digital platform-based funding mechanisms. Our findings highlight the role of regulation as a triggering enabler (Davidsson et al., 2018) for the adoption of novel funding mechanisms. Finally, we contribute to the literature on openness (e.g., Hautz et al., 2017; Stanko and Henard, 2017) by identifying the need to complement 'open' funding practices with open strategy and innovation practices, to make crowd-investor capabilities and networks accessible for entrepreneurs.

Practically, our results have implications for start-ups making choices about financing, for regulators that need to balance investor protection against the effectiveness of the financial system, and for operators of equity crowdfunding platforms who need to ensure that high-quality companies use their platforms going forward such that equity crowdfunding will not end up being a 'market for lemons'.

4 How Industry Specialisation Affects Venture Capitalists' Deal Selection and Value-added

The essay presented in this chapter addresses Research Question 2. It shall contribute to a more granular understanding of selection and treatment effects in VC financing by analysing venture capitalists' industry specialisation as an antecedent for their investment selection and value-added. The first section, 4.1, reviews the literature, and Section 4.2 derives the hypotheses. Section 4.3 elaborates on the dataset, variables, and empirical methodology. Section 4.4 presents the empirical analyses and results. Section 4.5 presents a discussion of the results and the limitations of this research. Finally, Section 4.6 sets forth the conclusions.[14,15]

4.1 Literature Review

4.1.1 Literature on VC Investment Selection and Value-added

The question as to whether VC investors add value to their investments beyond the provision of capital has long been disputed by academics in the research field of entrepreneurial finance (Gompers and Lerner, 2001; Baum and Silverman, 2004). This question is significant because investors

---

14 This chapter is largely based on a joint working paper with Professor Carolin Bock (Technische Universität Darmstadt) and Professor Massimiliano Guerini (Politecnico di Milano) and it is thus written from the first-person-plural point of view (i.e., *we*) in order to indicate that the research also reflects the opinions of the co-authors. A version of the working paper titled 'Disentangling investor value-add: How venture capitalists' specialization and investor-firm-fit affect venture capital value-add' was presented in a refereed paper session at the 2019 BCERC conference at Babson College, Babson Park, MA, USA in June 2019. Moreover, a version of the working paper titled 'Disentangling investor value-add: How VC specialization and investor-firm-fit affect VC value-add' was presented at the Third Entrepreneurial Finance Conference (ENTFIN) at Politecnico di Milano, in Milan, Italy in June 2018.

15 The working paper that forms the basis of this chapter received support from the 'RISIS Research infrastructures for the assessment of science, technology and innovation policy' project, funded by the European Union under the Seventh Framework Program (Grant Agreement n°313082).

and portfolio companies are not randomly matched (Tykvová, 2018) and it has been argued that VC investors are able to 'pick' superior companies while adding non-financial value to these companies following the investment (Amit et al., 1998; Hellmann and Puri, 2002; Baum and Silverman, 2004). Consequently, disentangling these two effects is of value to the empirical research on the topic. Extant research clearly focuses on the identification of the treatment effect, and the selection effect (also called the 'screening effect') is not typically evaluated explicitly (Tykvová, 2018). There are some exceptions.

For instance, Chemmanur et al. (2011) find that there is a selection effect as VC investors invest in companies which are more productive and possess more human capital (i.e. higher-paid employees). Their findings indicate that, nonetheless, VC investors are able to improve the efficiency of their portfolio companies. Consequently, these companies exhibit greater productivity growth than their non-VC-backed peers. Puri and Zarutskie (2011) report that VC-backed companies exhibit stronger revenue growth than non-backed companies that are otherwise comparable. They conclude that VC investors stimulate growth in their portfolio companies. While the two aforementioned studies employ different datasets from the US Census Bureau, Bertoni et al. (2011) and Croce et al. (2013) study similar research questions in a European context. Bertoni et al. (2011) do not find any evidence of a selection effect but, instead, demonstrate that investment by VC investors triggers strong employment and sales growth in new technology-based companies. Moreover, Croce et al. (2013), in contrast to Chemmanur et al. (2011), do not find evidence of differences in productivity growth prior to the receipt of VC financing (i.e. no selection effect) but report a significant treatment effect that even 'imprints' the portfolio companies, such that the higher productivity growth is maintained even after the exit of the VC. Taken together, these studies provide sound and robust empirical evidence of a positive causal treatment effect by VC investors on the growth and performance of their portfolio companies. The evidence regarding a selection effect is inconclusive.

It is important to note that the current understanding of whether a selection or a treatment effect prevails does not allow for inferences about potential differences *within* the group of VC-backed companies. For instance, the notion of 'screening', as employed by Chemmanur et al. (2011) and Croce et al. (2013), uses observable company-specific characteristics (for example, data about company revenues and cost structure) prior to the receipt of the initial VC funding in order to analyse whether VC-funded companies differ from non-funded companies. Thus, the empirical design of these papers compares VC-funded companies to non-funded companies but does not evaluate the differences *among* VC-funded companies. Consequently, prior research does not allow for inferences about whether *VC investors' ability to select promising ventures is heterogeneous* amongst VC investors (i.e. whether some VC investors are better at selecting portfolio companies than others). Our underlying assumption is that VC investors do differ in their ability to select promising ventures and that the degree of specialisation may affect this ability.

We further argue that it is insufficient to compare ventures based on observable company characteristics when evaluating potential differences among investors in terms of their ability to select high-potential companies. Specifically, we argue that the art of selecting promising companies is to detect their hidden potential, something that is not correctly perceived by other investors – such as future market opportunities (Chan, 1983; Tyebjee and Bruno, 1984; Amit et al., 1998). However, objective facts, such as accounting data (e.g., sales or productivity growth in the year prior to the investment round), are presumably available to other VC investors in the market at the time of the investment origination and, therefore, a VC investor cannot gain a competitive advantage by using these characteristics as the basis for decision-making. It is important to note that the literature does delineate the processes through and criteria on which VC investors base their investment decisions (e.g., Kirsch et al., 2009; Petty and Gruber, 2011). However, these studies do not link their understanding of the decision-making process to the 'quality' of the decision-making outcomes, which means they do not explain whether investors differ in their ability to select promising ventures. Consequently, potential causal factors for this alleged heterogeneity amongst investors remain unclear.

With regard to investor value-added (i.e. the treatment effect), several works build on the advances outlined above (Chemmanur et al., 2011; Bertoni et al., 2011; Croce et al., 2013) and have started to investigate which investor characteristics affect the value-added by investors (i.e. how investors create value). However, this research avenue has hitherto focused on different investor types (e.g., Chemmanur et al., 2014; Grilli and Murtinu, 2014; Guerini and Quas, 2016), while evidence regarding other causal factors remains scarce. The work by Krishnan et al. (2011) is one of the rare exceptions to this. They find that more reputable investors select higher-quality companies and that their reputation has a significant value-adding effect on ventures' post-IPO performance (Krishnan et al., 2011). Regarding the differences among investor types, Chemmanur et al. (2014) report that ventures backed by CVCs are more innovative but less profitable than those companies funded by IVCs, which – according to the authors – suggests that these ventures may benefit from the greater industry knowledge of their investors and that CVCs may be less sensitive to failure. Comparing GVCs and IVCs in Europe, Grilli and Murtinu (2014) find that IVCs have a significant positive impact on the sales growth of their portfolio companies, while GVCs provide only a negligible value-adding effect. Hence, the authors question the ability of governments to support high-tech ventures through GVC activities. Notwithstanding, Guerini and Quas (2016) report evidence suggesting that GVCs are able to select promising companies and to certify them to private VC investors which, in turn, invest in subsequent financing rounds.

To sum up, extant literature on VC selection and value-added has found that investors add value to their portfolio companies. Additionally, there is mixed evidence suggesting investors invest in companies which are ex ante of higher quality than companies that do not receive VC funding. However, the antecedents of selection and value-adding capabilities are not well understood and, therefore, little is known about the potential heterogeneity amongst the ability of investors to identify high-potential companies and provide non-financial value to them. As outlined earlier, our underlying assumption is that the specialisation of investors is an important determinant of both selection and value-adding capabilities. In order to link the literature stream about VC screening and value-addition with the literature on specialisation, we will thus review the literature on specialisation explicitly and highlight some deficiencies that need to be addressed.

4.1.2 Literature on Specialisation

Empirical research on VC specialisation finds contradictory results regarding its impact on the performance of VC investors and portfolio companies. On the one hand, certain studies report that specialisation is beneficial for VC investors' performance. For example, Gompers et al. (2009) report that greater investor specialisation (at both the individual and the VC firm level) results in higher performance for VC investors, when measured by the portfolio rate of exits (IPO, registration or acquisitions) in a given year. De Clercq and Dimov (2006) find lower portfolio failure rates for specialised VC investors and, in a related work, De Clercq and Dimov (2008) state that greater prior industry experience improves investment performance, as reflected by the status of companies (at the reference date of their study). Moreover, Lungeanu and Zajac (2016) document a positive relationship between investor industry experience and VC-company fit and IPO outcomes. Cressy et al. (2014) find that industry diversification reduces VC investors' fund performance in terms of successful IPOs. Additionally, early survey-based studies point in the same direction. In their pioneering paper, Sapienza et al. (1996) report that VC investors' industry experience is positively associated with value-added. That being said, when discussing this finding, it is important to point out that the authors' measure for value-added essentially captures the subjective value-added that investors attribute to themselves. Building on these works, Manigart et al. (2006) argue that non-specialised investors are less likely to add value to ventures (relying instead on their syndicate partners to do so), as they lack industry-specific knowledge. However, the empirical results of their survey do not support this notion. This may be explained by the fact that the authors 'rely on a crude measure of specialisation' (Manigart et al., 2006, p. 148).

On the other hand, several papers find that fund diversification improves investor performance. For example, Humphery-Jenner (2012) documents a positive relationship between industry diversification and the fund's internal rates of return (IRR) and Knill (2009) finds that increased diversification results in VC managers subsequently raising more follow-up capital. These results both suggest that diversification improves performance, since past performance is expected to positively influence fundraising. Buchner et al. (2017) find that diversified funds outperform specialist funds with respect to their IRR as diversification induces fund managers to endogenously pick riskier investments. Matusik and Fitza (2012) report a non-linear relationship between investor specialisation and portfolio IPO rates, as both highly specialised and highly diversified VC investors achieve more exits.

The inconclusive nature of the extant research may result from the several shortcomings that are present within the studies. Firstly, almost all the existing studies (De Clercq and Dimov, 2006; Gompers et al., 2009; Humphery-Jenner, 2012; Matusik and Fitza, 2012; Cressy et al., 2014) analyse outcomes at the portfolio level of the VC investors rather than the company (i.e. venture) level. This is interesting for several reasons, not least of all because analyses at the portfolio level are hampered by the effects stemming from differing levels of diversification (i.e. the reduction of idiosyncratic risk) (Ewens et al., 2013; Buchner et al., 2017) which impact performance at the portfolio level. Hence, when observing only portfolio returns, one cannot disentangle those performance differences that stem from mere portfolio diversification from those that may be caused by the influence of investors' diversification on their portfolio companies through value-adding activities.

Second, as Buchner et al. (2017) show, greater fund diversification not only reduces fund risk but the reduced fund risk endogenously induces investment managers to select riskier investments in the first place and, thus, investments with higher expected returns that result in greater portfolio performance for diversified investors. Moreover, as shown by Lungeanu and Zajac (2016), it is important to account for the *fit* between the experiential resources of investors and the needs of the individual portfolio company. Thus, a longitudinal analysis at the company (i.e. venture) level is indisputably required, as the investor–company-fit cannot be reflected at the portfolio level. We therefore account for the investor–company-fit by employing an established measure, borrowed from research on private equity buyouts by Cressy et al. (2007), for specialisation. This reflects the fit of investors' specialised expertise relevant to the venture at hand and will be discussed and defined in further detail in Section 4.3.3.

As previously outlined, it is necessary to account for endogeneity in this context to disentangle selection arising from the treatment effects which are generally a prevalent feature in the VC context (Baum and Silverman, 2004; Bertoni et al., 2011; Chemmanur et al., 2011; Croce et al., 2013). The findings of Buchner et al. (2017) further underscore this need in the context of research on specialisation, as several of the prior papers fail to do so (Gompers et al., 2009; Matusik and Fitza, 2012). For instance, the differences between VC investors in terms of their specialised experiential knowledge are very likely to affect their ability to select promising ventures (Gompers et al., 2009), which, in turn, is likely to involve unobservable company characteristics that vary over time, such as the quality and composition of the management team or the levels of market competition. Hence, advanced empirical methodologies are required to draw *causal* inferences about the value-adding capabilities of specialist investors and to separate these effects from selection effects. We respond to this need by introducing robust regression techniques, namely the two-step system generalised method of moments (GMM-SYS) approach (Arellano and Bover, 1995; Blundell and Bond, 1998).

Finally, many prior studies use only partial (i.e. coarse) measures for success, such as IPO rates, IPO outcomes or the status of companies at a single point in time (De Clercq and Dimov, 2008; Matusik and Fitza, 2012; Lungeanu and Zajac, 2016). These approaches, driven by the scarcity of data on private companies, are limited by the samples being composed exclusively of IPO companies as this causes the results to be impacted by selection bias (Bertoni et al., 2011) and because the status of a venture at a single point in time is a crude measure for performance. Moreover, given that our study contemplates early-stage financing within the European ecosystem, reliance on IPO outcomes is particularly problematic as IPO markets in Europe are less liquid than those in the US and IPOs are infrequent (Black and Gilson, 1998; Schwienbacher, 2008; Hege et al., 2009). We therefore advocate the use of time-series data and operational measures for company performance (for instance, sales growth), just as prior researchers in the field of VC value-added in the European context have concluded (Bertoni et al., 2011; Croce et al., 2013; Guerini and Quas, 2016).

Taken together, the review of the literature on investor selection and value-added and the literature on VC specialisation suggests that specialisation may affect VC investors' selection and value-adding capabilities. However, the inconclusive and limited empirical evidence on the effects of investor specialisation warrants further examination using data better suited to the task and more advanced methodologies. Our analysis on the consequences of investor specialisation provides an important contribution, as it disentangles selection and treatment effects, accounts for the investor–company-fit, and employs a longitudinal dataset of company operating performance in the context of European companies.

4.2 Hypotheses Development

As discussed extensively above, VC investors act as both 'scouts' that aim to select the most promising companies to invest in and as 'coaches' that aim to improve these companies (Baum and Silverman, 2004; Croce et al., 2013). Hence, it is important to assess whether and how specialisation and investor–company-fit affect these vital capabilities and whether it can explain heterogeneity among investors regarding differences in their ability to select high-potential companies and add value to them. In this section, we will derive our hypotheses separately for selection and value-added and start, following the investment process, with the selection capabilities.

Entrepreneurial ventures are particularly difficult to finance for a number of reasons, including their highly uncertain future development, the inherent information problems and the absence of tangible assets available to be used as risk-reducing collateral (Amit et al., 1998). As a consequence, VC investors have adopted individual, subjective and contingent methods to inform their decision-making (e.g., Kirsch et al., 2009; Petty and Gruber, 2011) regarding their investment in young ventures (Drover et al.,

2017). Given the strong information problems, increased specialisation may help investors reduce informational asymmetries – for instance, Gompers et al. (2009) argue that specialised VC investors may become industry experts who possess a superior understanding of technology, markets and people. Greater expertise would then lead to better investments within an industry. Accordingly, Gompers et al. (2009) argue that specialisation equips VC investors with superior selection capabilities. Similarly, the findings of Manigart et al. (2006) support the notion that early-stage investors that are industry-specialised face lower information asymmetries when assessing investment opportunities (and therefore have a lower propensity to syndicate for screening purposes), resulting in superior selection capabilities. Thus, we formulate:

Hypothesis 1: Specialised investors select companies with greater inherent growth potential than non-specialised investors.

While it is well established that VC investors are actively involved in their investments and provide their portfolio companies with a variety of value-adding activities – including strategic and managerial support (Gorman and Sahlman, 1989; Sahlman, 1990) – the effects of greater specialisation on investor value-added are not sufficiently documented, as outlined above. Prior findings document that certain investors may have more expertise and therefore may add more value than others while also suggesting that the expertise of VC investors is a potentially valuable resource that can be transferred to portfolio companies (Lungeanu and Zajac, 2016). However, it is not trivial to define ex ante in which direction specialised expertise may affect investor value-added – i.e. whether drawing from deep industry knowledge or a diverse background is more beneficial to investors.

On the one hand, as described above, several papers report positive effects stemming from VC investors' specialisation and investor–company-fit on the performance of VC portfolios and/or portfolio companies (e.g., De Clercq and Dimov, 2006; Lungeanu and Zajac, 2016). Moreover, related research from the adjacent field of private equity, namely the research undertaken by Cressy et al. (2007), asserts that increased specialisation confers a competitive advantage for buyout transactions and finds that the post-investment performance of companies acquired by specialised investors is superior to that of its peers. Indeed, there are several theoretical arguments that support the view that specialised expertise should improve the value-adding capabilities of VC investors. First, more specialised industry expertise and greater investor–company-fit facilitate the monitoring of portfolio companies by the VC investors. As specialised investors possess a comprehensive understanding of the industry and the ventures of businesses therein, they may detect potential problems, misbehaviour or deteriorating venture performance more easily and may, therefore, correct them more quickly (Gupta and Sapienza, 1992; Norton and Tenenbaum,1993; De Clercq and Dimov, 2006). Second, as VC investors create value for their portfolio companies by detecting potential threats and opportunities in the business environment (Hsu, 2006), in-depth knowledge of the industry and environment could certainly facilitate this task. Third, greater specialisation allows for improved information sharing between investments (Norton and Tenenbaum, 1993) and the insights acquired from one particular venture can be useful in the management of other similar ventures in the portfolio (De Clercq et al., 2001). This notion is in line with the organisational learning perspective proposed by Matusik and Fitza (2012), according to which the specialised knowledge possessed by VC investors allows for lower coordination costs and more efficient information processing. Therefore, we formulate:

Hypothesis 2 a: Specialised investors have a positive treatment effect on venture performance compared to non-specialised investors.

However, given the variance among the findings of prior research on specialisation vs. diversification as an investment strategy, an alternative standpoint is equally plausible. As mentioned, several studies have reported that diversified VC funds show superior performance over non-diversified (i.e. specialised) funds, which may hint at advantages stemming from diversification. With regard to theoretical benefits from diversification for the effectiveness of investors' value-added services, Matusik and Fitza (2012) argue that a diversified VC investor acquires a diverse knowledge stock that enables it to better solve complex problems and to create novel solutions, as diverse knowledge stocks improve problem-solving skills (Ahuja and Katila, 2001) and foster analogical thinking (Gavetti et al., 2005). A VC investor with a diverse background (i.e. knowledge stock) also acquires the ability to advise a portfolio company on different possible trajectories – which is a valuable capability given that early-stage companies are dynamic and might change the scope of their operations, for example by applying their technology in a different industry setting as exemplified by Matusik and Fitza (2012). In a similar vein, Humphery-Jenner (2013) argues that diversification improves fund performance due to knowledge sharing and learning across investments. Specialisation and greater investor–company-fit may bring detrimental effects, namely a greater likelihood of knowledge appropriation, because the investor has a better understanding of the venture's business and is, therefore, more likely to link this knowledge with competing ventures in the portfolio (see Katila et al., 2008 for knowledge appropriation in context of CVC, and Ueda, 2004 for the role of knowledge appropriation in a theoretical comparison of VC investors and banks). As shown by Pahnke et al. (2015), in order to optimise its portfolio returns, a VC investor may intentionally leak information from one portfolio company to its competitor if the VC investor is invested in both companies (i.e. it may be better for a VC investor to realise one large exit than several smaller ones as returns are highly skewed). Pahnke et al. (2015) find evidence suggesting that the leakage of competitive information harms innovation by ventures (as measured by the number of product introductions by ventures in the medical device industry). Moreover, even if VC investors abide by these practices, their portfolio companies may nonetheless anticipate such information appropriating-behaviour and establish defences in response (Katila et al., 2008). For instance, they may hold back relevant information, harming the working relationship between VC investors and their portfolio companies, and causing detriment to investor value-added, too. Therefore, we propose the following alternative hypothesis:

Hypothesis 2 b: Specialised investors have a negative treatment effect on venture performance compared to non-specialised investors.

As the needs (Lungeanu and Zajac, 2016) and interaction intensity between VC investors and portfolio companies (Sapienza et al., 1996) vary throughout the development of a company, it is important to account for companies' maturity as a potential moderator. Again, there are several plausible alternative standpoints.

On the one hand, early-stage companies are more difficult to monitor than more mature companies given that uncertainty, risk and information asymmetries are higher in the earlier stages of financing (Sapienza et al., 1996; Plummer et al., 2015). Hence, it is likely to be particularly beneficial for VC investors' if they can draw on specialised expertise to detect potential issues or deteriorating venture performance and initiate corrective actions faster for portfolio companies in their early-developmental stages (Gupta and Sapienza, 1992; Norton and Tenenbaum, 1993; De Clercq and Dimov, 2006). Moreover, when it comes to the detection of threats and opportunities present in the business environment (Hsu, 2006), scenarios for which VC investors' specialised expertise seems particularly valuable, one would again expect a stronger effect for early-stage companies given that these companies typically experience resource constraints and, thus, do not have the capacity to undertake extensive efforts in areas such as market intelligence or strategy. Hence, we formulate:

Hypothesis 3 a: The positive treatment effect that specialised investors have on venture performance compared to non-specialised investors is greater if the venture is in an earlier development stage.

However, the benefits of diversification identified in the organisational learning literature are also expected to be more pronounced for younger companies than for those that are more mature (Matusik and Fitza, 2012). For instance, it is widely accepted that entrepreneurs leading early-stage companies often need to utilise experimental or trial and error strategy processes in order to iteratively determine how to position their company and how best to compete in the given context (Nicholls-Nixon et al., 2000). Hence, the strategy and positioning of early-stage companies is more likely to change over time. The less mature a company is, the more helpful it is if a VC investor can advise the company on different possible trajectories. This is one benefit that VC investors with a diverse knowledge stock bring to a portfolio company, according to Matusik and Fitza (2012). In the same vein, younger companies are also more likely to be confronted with complex novel problems which have not yet been solved by other companies – in which case the benefits of a diverse knowledge stock (problem solving, analogical thinking) are more pronounced (Matusik and Fitza, 2012). On top of that, the risk of knowledge appropriation is greater for young companies, as these companies are likely to possess fewer defences, whilst being more vulnerable to competitors and VC investors (Pahnke et al., 2015). Hence, we propose the following alternative hypothesis:

Hypothesis 3 b: The negative treatment effect that specialised investors have on venture performance compared to non-specialised investors is greater if the venture is in an earlier development stage.

4.3 Variables, Sample and Methodology

4.3.1 Dataset and Sample Construction

We test our hypotheses by an empirical analysis based on a sample of VC investments extracted from the VICO 4.0 dataset, which has been created as a part of the RISIS research project promoted by the European Commission (see http://risis.eu for details) under the Seventh Framework Program.

The dataset contains geographical, industry and accounting information on 24,238 companies that i) have received at least one initial equity investment (e.g., VC, angel finance, crowdfunding) starting from 1 January 1998 up to the end of 2014, ii) have been incorporated after 1 January 1988 and iii) are located in a EU-28 country or Israel. Companies were selected through three different proprietary datasets: Thompson One Private Equity, Zephyr, and Crunchbase. Thomson One Private Equity is the main source of information, accounting for 17,286 companies. However, the inclusion of companies from Zephyr and Crunchbase allowed us to increase the coverage of the dataset by 40% (6,952 additional companies).

For each company, the complete outside equity financial history as it is reported in the three abovementioned sources is tracked up to 2014. At the investment deal level, VICO 4.0 provides information on the deal date, the total amount invested, the number and the type of investors. Detailed information has been also collected for each company and investor, including company's and investor's industry sector, address, foundation date, company's exit (IPO or acquisition), and finally company's accounting information (source: ORBIS database). The dataset contains 8,761 distinct investors. Companies and investors have been involved in 38,112 investment deals.

For this research, we focus on companies which have received a first-round investment from European VC investors between 2003 and 2014 and were younger than 10 years old at investment date.[16] To be precise, we focus only on companies involved in VC investments, discarding crowdfunding and business angels deals. Furthermore, we do not consider companies which received funding from non-European investors, as we are not able to assess these investors' track record and specialisation (please see Section 4.3.3 for details on the specialisation measures). Moreover, we include only companies for which the available accounting data allows us to assess at least three years of company performance in our regressions, in order to properly compute the panel-data econometric estimators used in this work (see Section 4.3).

After applying the abovementioned criteria and dropping missing observations, our final regression sample includes 8,308 company-year observa-

---

16 We require that companies be no more than 10 years old when raising their first round of capital, as we aim to analyse the effects of investor specialization in the context of high-growth early-stage start-ups rather than buyout companies.

tions from 1,459 companies, i.e. for each company the time series spans on average 5.7 years.

4.3.2 Dependent Variable Definitions

We use turnover growth as the dependent variable to proxy for VC investors' value-adding capabilities at the operational level and define it in a manner analogous to the related research by Grilli and Murtinu (2014): turnover growth at time (t) equals the natural logarithmic company growth between time (t-1) and (t) (i.e. $\ln(\text{Turnover}_{i,t}) - \ln(\text{Turnover}_{i,t-1})$). Using company growth is helpful because it allows us to track the performance of these companies and the value-added by investors consistently and continuously. This is otherwise not possible using coarse event-based variables, such as company status or IPO outcomes (variables which have been relied on in related research by, for instance, De Clercq and Dimov, 2008; Matusik and Fitza, 2012; and Lungeanu and Zajac, 2016). Moreover, given that we consider the early-stage financing ecosystem within Europe, operating performance is well suited for tracking company development, since IPO markets in Europe are less liquid than those in the US and, thus, VC exits via IPOs are less frequent (Black and Gilson, 1998; Schwienbacher, 2008; Hege et al., 2009).

4.3.3 Independent Variable Definitions

The key variable of interest is our measure for investor specialisation. Using related literature, we have identified two archetypical approaches to measure and analyse investor specialisation. In the following, we will discuss them whilst describing our corresponding variables in detail.

The first measure requires separate analysis for each company, as it jointly accounts for VC investor specialisation and the *fit* of this specialisation to the focal venture. Cressy et al. (2007) detail a specialisation metric that assesses the degree of investor specialisation within a specific industry in which the focal company (which is funded by the investor at hand) operates. This procedure is particularly helpful for inferences about the effect of specialisation at the *company* level, as it accounts for the fact that companies' needs differ and that the value of VC investors' specialised expertise depends on the context in which it is applied (see Lungeanu and Zajac, 2016). We build on the related research on private equity buyout transactions by Cressy et al. (2007) and define specialisation accordingly as an index of competitive advantage (ICA) – a construct that is based on the literature on international trade and technological specialisation (Archibugi and Pianta, 1994). Similar to the definition proposed by Cressy et al. (2007), we define *ICA* for the VC sector as:

$$ICA_{i,t,y} = (F_{ity}/F_{.ty})/(F_{it}/F_{.t})$$

where:

F_{ity} is the number of companies in industry y that VC investor i funded during the period t-5 to t-0;

$F_{.ty}$ is the total number of companies in industry y that all VC investors funded during the period t-5 to t-0;

F_{it} is the total number of companies that VC investor i funded during the period t-5 to t-0; and

$F_{.t}$ is the total number of companies that all VC investors funded during the period t-5 to t-0.

The numerator of *ICA* represents the share of a VC investor in all investments within an industry and the denominator captures its share of all investments made within the market. For each investor in period t, we consider the investment track record from t-5 to t-0 to calculate the *ICA* for each industry. This means that the industry *ICA* of an investor is time-variant.[17] If an investment is syndicated, we take the average *ICA* in the syndicate as a proxy for the joint expertise of the syndicate.[18] Moreover, we only consider those investors which are active in the most recent financing round of the start-up. So, for example, if an investor contributes to the first financing round of a venture, but not to the second, we disregard the investor from the second round onwards. The implicit assumption behind this method is that, if an investor does not invest in follow-on rounds, it is also less likely to engage in value-adding activities. Further, given the importance of meaningful indus-

---

17 If an investor has completed less than 10 investments overall, *ICA* is set to 0, since the investor's track record is insufficient to assess its specialization and we do not want to conflate specialization with inexperience.

18 By using an average, the calculation implicitly weighs investors' influence in a syndicate commensurate to their degree of specialization. We challenge this assumption and provide a robustness check in Section 6, in which we do not use the *average ICA* of a syndicate as determinant for the overall syndicate specialization but rather employ the *share of specialized* investors in a syndicate as a metric.

try classifications that reflect the specific expertise and knowledge through which investors add value, we manually aggregate the NACE-industries into more thematic categories (for example, medical/health/life sciences) and use these for the *ICA* calculation as well as for all other specialisation metrics. Further, building on *ICA*, and also following Cressy et al. (2007), we define a dummy variable, *Specialisation*, that is equal to 1 if $ICA_{i,t,y}$ is greater than 1 (i.e. if a VC firm invests in an industry in which its past investment share is greater than the overall market share), and 0 otherwise. Hence, *Specialisation* captures both the relative specialisation of a VC investor and the fit of its expertise to the relevant venture, and its coefficient thus provides a measure for the value-added that these specialised investors provide to companies located within their field of specialisation.

In order to explore the effects of specialisation in more detail, we further divide *Specialisation* into *Strong specialisation* and *Moderate specialisation*. *Strong specialisation* is a dummy equal to 1 if the *modified ICA* of an investor is greater than 1. The calculation of the *modified ICA* differs from the standard *ICA* in the following way: A VC firm's share of all investments in an industry is compared to its share in investments completed by investors who have invested in the given industry during the calculation period instead of being compared to its share in the overall VC market (as it is the case for the standard *ICA*). The idea is to use a narrower definition of the relevant comparable 'market' (i.e. the relevant peer group of VC investors active in the focal industry) in response to the observation that the majority of VC investors specialise in certain areas; thereby creating a scenario where it might not be sufficient to measure an investor's relative degree of specialisation in terms of the overall market average. Hence, we define *Strong specialisation* in order to identify those investors (or syndicates)[19] which are specialised relative to the relevant subsample of investors, namely those peers that have invested in the same industry in the past. *Moderate specialisation* is equal to 1 in all other cases – i.e. if an investor's (or syndicate's) standard *ICA* is greater than 1 but the modified *ICA* is less than 1 – or, in other words, if an investor is specialised relative to the overall market but less specialised than its peers.

The second measure of specialisation does not account for investor–company-fit and, instead, captures the overall effect that specialisation has across all investments in a VC investor's portfolio. For instance, both Buchner et al. (2017) and Dimov and De Clercq (2006) employ the Herfindahl-Hirschman-

---

19 As in the case of *ICA*, the *modified ICA* of a syndicate is defined as the average *modified ICA* of all investors involved in the syndicate.

Index (*HHI*) to measure concentration within an investor's portfolio as this reflects the degree to which investors have adopted a narrow investment focus in the past. In contrast to the *Specialisation* dummy, a VC investor's portfolio *HHI* is independent of a(n) (investee) company's industry and thus provides a proxy for the *overall* value-added by investors following a specialisation strategy. Put differently, the *HHI* only captures a VC's portfolio concentration and then measures the effect on value-added across investments. In order to simplify the interpretation of the coefficient and to ensure the results are comparable to those obtained using the *Specialisation* dummy (i.e. measurement of whether the portfolio concentration is high *relative* to the other investors), we define the *Concentration* dummy as equal to 1 if the *HHI* of an investor (or the average *HHI* in a syndicate) is greater than the median *HHI* in our sample. For further comparability, we calculate the *HHI* using the same timeframe and industry classifications as the *ICA*.

4.3.4 Other Independent Variables and Controls

To test Hypothesis 2, we define two further independent variables of interest. The first is *Round number*, which is the number of financing rounds a company has raised up to the focal year. This variable proxies for the developmental stage of a company, as the provision of external capital by investors is typically staged and tied to the realisation of certain milestones. The second variable, *Age,* captures a company's age in years.[20]

Our control variables include the natural logarithm of the lagged levels of turnover (*l.ln(Turnover)*) and the location (i.e. nation) of the company to control for institutional differences among companies, as well as year dummies which capture general macroeconomic conditions. Moreover, to rule out the possibility that specialisation is conflated with inexperience or smaller scale, we control for investor experience using the natural logarithm of the total number of deals an investor (or syndicate) has completed during the rolling period over which we calculate our specialisation metrics (*ln(Past deals)*). Additionally, the dichotomous variable *Syndicate* controls for the presence of more than one investor in the past financing round given that syndication has been found to affect value-added (Tian, 2012). Finally, we control for industry.

---

20 Given that *Age* and *Round number* are likely to show correlations, it is worth noting that we check for the correlation of all our variables and variance inflation factors – details are outlined in Section 4.3.3.

4.3.5 Empirical Methodology

In order to test our research question empirically, we use three different empirical approaches: OLS regressions, fixed effects (FE) regressions and two-step system generalised method of moments regressions (GMM-SYS).

OLS is a preliminary estimation strategy in the sense that it accounts for a variety of covariates but does not address the concern that unobserved company characteristics may influence decision-making by specialised VC investors and the company's growth performance. Given our hypotheses, we expect this kind of effect – but if it were the case, our independent variables would be rendered endogenous and their coefficients would be biased and inconsistent. Hence, caution is required when interpreting the OLS results and more robust techniques are called for. As a first step, the FE estimation tackles any potential concerns on the endogeneity of independent variables that would be caused by their (alleged) correlation with unobservable factors that are constant over time.

However, the characteristics that may cause endogeneity issues in the receipt of financing from specialised VC investors are likely to vary over time, given that the young high-growth companies in our sample are very dynamic. For instance, the 'value proposition' of the business model or the 'capabilities' of the management team can be used as potential examples of such time-variant factors. Moreover, the companies also typically receive value-adding contributions from different investors over time. As a consequence, both OLS and FE estimators are expected to be biased, because we are unable to observe certain company characteristics that are likely to influence both decision-making by specialised VC investors and the company's growth performance. Therefore, we resort to the GMM-SYS approach (Arellano and Bover, 1995; Blundell and Bond, 1998) to address the endogeneity of VC investments.

We use GMM-SYS with finite-sample correction (Windmeijer, 2005)[21] and implement it using a software package provided by Roodman (2006). This approach is econometrically highly robust and practically established within the literature on VC investor value-added (e.g., Croce et al., 2013;

---

21 Although the employed two-step estimator is asymptotically more efficient than the alternative one-step variant, the reported two-step standard errors are typically downward biased (Arellano and Bond, 1991; Blundell and Bond, 1998). Therefore, in all GMM regressions, we apply the finite-sample correction for the two-step covariance matrix that was suggested by Windmeijer (2005) for this case and which Roodman (2006) makes available in his software package.

Grilli and Murtinu, 2014) and in related fields of entrepreneurial finance research (e.g., Samila and Sorenson, 2011). In the GMM-SYS analyses, we use the lags of the periods t-3 to t-5 as instruments for the potentially endogenous VC investor and company characteristics. The start in t-3 is justified by the results of the Arellano-Bond tests AR1–AR3 (please refer to the respective regression tables for the exact test statistics), showing that from the third lag onwards, no autocorrelation is observed which would otherwise disqualify these lags as valid instruments (Roodman, 2009). We limit the number of lags to t-5 in order to avoid finite-sample bias, which could be caused by a number of instruments that is too large (Roodman, 2009; for the application in related research see Grilli and Murtinu, 2014). Finally, we routinely test the validity of our overidentifying restrictions, i.e. the exogeneity of our instruments, using the Hansen J-statistic.

The advantage of employing different identification strategies, including the inferior OLS regression, is that potential differences between the different regression models are interpretable and allow for inferences on selection effects. We will discuss this in more detail in Section 4.4.

4.4 Analyses and Results

4.4.1 Sample Overview and Univariate Tests

Our final sample includes 8,308 company-year-observations from 1,459 companies and covers a variety of different industries (see Table 15). Unsurprisingly, the software, communications and media, and medical/healthcare/life sciences industries represent the largest industries and account for 43% of the companies altogether. This share is in line with our expectations, as these industries are at the heart of start-up activity. Accordingly, it is highly plausible that fewer companies stem from the other represented industries, such as real estate or agriculture.

Moreover, the sample includes 25 EU countries (i.e. all EU member states except Cyprus, Luxembourg and Malta) and Israel, such that the sample covers the vast majority of the European start-up ecosystem. It is noteworthy, however, that differences in national regulations drive the proliferation of accounting data, such that certain countries, like France and Sweden, are more strongly represented than others, like Germany (see Table 16). We address this phenomenon using a dedicated robustness check (see Section 4.5) in which we account for national differences in investor specialisation.

Table 15: Sample distribution by industry

Industry	Number of companies	Share
Software	314	21.5%
Communications and media	189	13.0%
Medical/health/life sciences	172	11.8%
Computers and electronic components	124	8.5%
Non high-tech manufacturing	120	8.2%
Machinery and equipment	72	4.9%
Consulting	54	3.7%
Finance and insurance	49	3.4%
R&D and engineering	48	3.3%
Support services	43	3.0%
Wholesale and retail trade	41	2.8%
Cultural and creative industries	35	2.4%
Chemicals	33	2.3%
Energy and environment	32	2.2%
Other non high-tech services	28	1.9%
Construction	23	1.6%
Aerospace	20	1.4%
Motor vehicles	17	1.2%
Trasportation	15	1.0%
Real estate	11	0.8%
Agriculture, forestry and fishing	10	0.7%
Sports	9	0.6%
Total	**1,459**	**100.0%**

Table 17 shows summary statistics and correlations for our regression variables. As there are few cases evidencing high correlation, we check the variance inflation factor (VIF) and find it to be well below 2 for our independent variables of interest and below 3 for the remaining variables (not reported for brevity). As such, we find no evidence that the regression analyses suffer from issues of multicollinearity (O'Brien, 2007; Wooldridge, 2009). Table 18 shows a univariate comparison between companies which, at any point in time, have received funding from specialist investors, and their peers. The analysis reveals that specialist-financed and generalist-financed companies are on average (i.e. across time) similar in terms of size and that they show similar levels of turnover growth. However, specialised investors invest in more mature companies, a fact which becomes particularly evident when the number of funding rounds are considered (Table 18). Moreover, it is interesting to note that most companies raise at least one round from specialised investors. Finally, it is evident that the companies in our sample are still in their early stages of development, as they have raised, on average, only 1 round of financing and are, across all observations in the panel, about 6 years old. These features are in line with our aim to analyse early-stage companies. In the next section, we will assess company growth and the respective investor value-added using more robust analyses.

Table 16: Sample distribution by country

Country	Number of companies	Share
Belgium	17	1%
Finland	113	8%
France	612	42%
Germany	85	6%
Italy	59	4%
Other countries	75	5%
Poland	25	2%
Portugal	18	1%
Spain	125	9%
Sweden	143	10%
United Kingdom	187	13%
Total	**1,459**	**100%**

Table 17: *Variable overview and correlation matrix*

Variable	Mean	SD	Median	Min	Max	1	2	3	4	5	6	7	8	9	10
1 ln(Turnover growth)	0.25	0.75	0.14	-1.49	2.84	1.00									
2 Specialisation	0.44	0.50	0.00	0.00	1.00	-0.04	1.00								
3 Portfolio concentration	0.37	0.48	0.00	0.00	1.00	-0.05	0.05	1.00							
4 Strong specialisation	0.29	0.45	0.00	0.00	1.00	-0.04	0.75	0.11	1.00						
5 Moderate specialisation	0.15	0.35	0.00	0.00	1.00	-0.01	0.49	-0.07	-0.22	1.00					
6 ln(Past deals)	2.58	1.66	2.89	0.00	6.54	-0.07	0.61	0.13	0.40	0.37	1.00				
7 Syndication	0.21	0.41	0.00	0.00	1.00	-0.03	0.18	0.25	0.10	0.12	0.43	1.00			
8 l.ln(Turnover)	7.05	2.51	7.24	0.00	11.55	-0.33	0.03	0.02	0.00	0.04	0.07	-0.03	1.00		
9 Age	6.75	3.80	6.00	1.00	21.00	-0.23	0.19	0.17	0.13	0.10	0.35	0.15	0.42	1.00	
10 Round number	1.15	0.94	1.00	0.00	10.00	-0.10	0.40	0.27	0.32	0.17	0.59	0.24	0.14	0.39	1.00

Table 18: *Univariate comparison of specialist-financed and non-specialist financed companies*

Variable	Non-specialist financed companies			Specialist-financed companies			Mean difference
	Obs.	Mean	SD	Obs.	Mean	SD	t-value
ln(Turnover)	2,366	7.30	2.42	5,942	7.32	2.38	-0.26
ln(Turnover growth)	2,366	0.25	0.73	5,942	0.26	0.75	-0.55
Age in years	2,366	6.63	3.78	5,942	6.80	3.81	-1.85*
Funding rounds	2,366	0.93	0.61	5,942	1.23	1.03	-13.55***

Table 18 shows an overview of our sample in the context of four variables and compares non-specialist financed companies and specialist-financed companies. Ln(Turnover) captures the natural logarithm of company turnover and ln(Turnover growth) accounts for natural logarithmic company growth between (t-1) and (t0).

4.4.2 Regression Analyses

In Table 19, we present our initial regression analyses. Columns 1 and 2 show OLS regressions in which *Specialisation* and *Portfolio concentration* are the central independent variables, and Columns 3 and 4 show the corresponding FE regressions. Surprisingly, the coefficient for *Specialisation* is insignificant in both regressions (Columns 1 and 3). Hence, we do not observe significant differences in the turnover growth of companies funded by specialist investors when ignoring potential selection (i.e. endogeneity) effects. However, the coefficient of *Portfolio concentration* is negative in the OLS regression (Column 2). Thus, when evaluating the performance of portfolio companies across investments (i.e. including potential investments outside their area of expertise), the companies backed by investors with a narrow investment focus (and a high industry portfolio concentration) show significantly lower turnover growth. The effect vanishes in the company FE regression (Column 4) which implies that the performance difference found in the OLS regression can be ascribed to unobservable time-invariant factors rather than to a causal treatment effect.

Table 19: OLS and FE regressions of turnover growth

Variable	(1) OLS	(2) OLS	(3) FE	(4) FE
Specialisation	-0.0232		-0.0156	
	(-1.246)		(-0.616)	
Portfolio concentration		-0.0367**		-0.00491
		(-2.169)		(-0.200)
ln(Past deals)	-0.00317	-0.00952	0.0342***	0.0315***
	(-0.473)	(-1.577)	(2.785)	(2.851)
Syndicate dummy	-0.0368*	-0.0220	-0.0227	-0.0194
	(-1.740)	(-1.017)	(-0.454)	(-0.387)
l.ln(Turnover)	-0.0969***	-0.0965***	-0.373***	-0.373***
	(-19.34)	(-19.30)	(-26.47)	(-26.47)
Age	-0.0138***	-0.0138***	0.0100	0.0101
	(-5.742)	(-5.752)	(1.546)	(1.557)
Round number	0.000560	0.00348	-0.00786	-0.00772
	(0.0586)	(0.357)	(-0.291)	(-0.274)
Constant	1.099***	1.124***	2.766***	2.767***
	(11.05)	(11.15)	(31.98)	(31.97)
R-squared	0.147	0.147	0.347	0.347
Country FE	YES	YES	NO	NO
Industry FE	YES	YES	NO	NO
Year FE	YES	YES	YES	YES
Company FE	NO	NO	YES	YES
N	8,308	8,308	8,308	8,308

Table 19 shows OLS and FE regressions of start-up turnover growth. Regressions 1 and 2 are standard OLS regressions with robust standard errors, Regressions 3 and 4 are FE regressions with company fixed effects and robust standard errors. *Specialisation* is a dummy variable equal to 1 if the *ICA* (average *ICA*) of an investor (investor syndicate) in a given year is >1 and is otherwise 0. *Portfolio concentration* is a dummy variable equal to 1 if the *HHI* (average *HHI*) of an investor (investor syndicate) exceeds the median *HHI* value in our sample. Further details and the definitions of the remaining variables are presented in Section 4.3. Robust z-statistics are reported in parentheses. *, ** and *** denote statistical significance at the 10%, 5% and 1% level, respectively.

While the FE regressions account for unobserved time-invariant heterogeneity among companies, GMM-SYS is the most robust technique, as the companies in our sample change over time and are exposed to value-adding activities by different investors over time. Therefore, as detailed in Section 4.3.3., GMM-SYS addresses the alleged endogeneity of our key explanatory variable and thus allows for causal inferences about the effects of investor specialisation on companies, i.e. investor value-added. The results of our GMM-SYS regressions are presented in Table 20. The coefficients for *Specialisation* and *Portfolio concentration* are both negative and significant – the former at the 5% level (Column 1) and the latter at the 1% level (Column 2). The significance of the coefficients suggests that raising an incremental round of financing (noting that we control for the number of rounds raised) from an investor (or an investment syndicate) which is specialised or has a high portfolio concentration affects turnover growth negatively compared to raising a round from an investor or syndicate which is not specialised and does not have a high portfolio concentration. Hence, we conclude that investor specialisation hampers the ability of those investors to add value to companies, which is in line with Hypothesis 2 b. The magnitude of the effect is also economically meaningful: the backing of a specialised VC investor leads to an 11.2% reduction in turnover growth, while the turnover growth of VC investors with a concentrated portfolio tends to be 13.3% lower than its peers (Table 20, Columns 1 and 2). Since the two specialisation measures are closely related, we bring them together in another regression (Column 3) in order to assess whether the two constructs have distinct effects. Although the magnitude of the coefficients decreases slightly, both remain negative at unchanged significance levels. Hence, narrower investment focus and greater relative specialisation and investor–company-fit harm investor value-added in distinct ways, as highlighted by the fact that the coefficients for both variables remain significant in the joint regression.

Moreover, it is worth comparing the results from the OLS regressions with those from the GMM-SYS regressions to draw inferences about selection effects. While the coefficient for *Specialisation* is not significantly different from 0 in the OLS regression (Table 4, Column 1), it is negative and significant in the GMM-SYS regression (Table 5, Column 1). Hence, even though specialised investors add less value to ventures (as evidenced by the GMM regressions), these ventures do not show any differences in growth according to the OLS regressions, which implies that specialised investors (with high investor–company fit) have selected companies with greater intrinsic growth potential. This finding is in line with Hypothesis 1. It is interesting to note that the findings for *Portfolio concentration* are slightly different in the sense that the coefficient in the OLS regression (Table 4, Column 2) is negative too, although it is smaller in size and shows a lower significance level than the coefficient in the GMM regression (Table 5, Column 2). Thus, the comparison between the findings of *Specialisation* and

Portfolio concentration suggests that investor–company-fit plays an important role for selection in the sense that it improves investors' selection capabilities beyond the (positive) effect of specialised expertise.

Table 20: GMM-SYS regressions of turnover growth

	(1)	(2)	(3)
Variable	GMM-SYS	GMM-SYS	GMM-SYS
Specialisation	-0.112**		-0.0956**
	(-2.275)		(-2.058)
Portfolio concentration		-0.133***	-0.123***
		(-2.633)	(-2.596)
ln(Past deals)	-0.0134	-0.0437**	-0.0274
	(-0.683)	(-2.467)	(-1.390)
Syndicate dummy	-0.0479	0.0331	0.00903
	(-0.905)	(0.574)	(0.162)
l.ln(Turnover)	-0.186***	-0.189***	-0.178***
	(-5.836)	(-5.933)	(-6.098)
Age	0.00914	0.0108	0.00757
	(1.112)	(1.324)	(0.996)
Round number	0.0108	0.0246	0.0270
	(0.503)	(1.289)	(1.493)
Constant	1.576***	1.609***	1.558***
	(10.13)	(10.69)	(11.18)
Country FE	YES	YES	YES
Industry FE	YES	YES	YES
Year FE	YES	YES	YES
AR1 p-value	0	0	0
AR2 p-value	0.00825	0.00729	0.00800
AR3 p-value	0.841	0.725	0.799
Hansen J-statistic p-value	0.239	0.226	0.308
N	8,308	8,308	8,308

Table 20 shows GMM-SYS regressions (two-step system generalised method of moments estimator) with finite-sample correction of start-up turnover growth. *Specialisation* is a dummy variable equal to 1 if the *ICA* (average *ICA*) of an investor (investor syndicate) in a given year is >1 and is otherwise 0. *Portfolio concentration* is a dummy variable equal to 1 if the *HHI* (average *HHI*) of an investor (investor syndicate) exceeds the median *HHI* value in our sample. Further details and the definitions of the remaining variables are presented in Section 4.3. Robust z-statistics are reported in parentheses. *, ** and *** denote statistical significance at the 10%, 5% and 1% level, respectively.

In order to obtain a more nuanced understanding of the findings on investor value-added, we investigate different levels of specialisation in Table 21. As described in Section 4.3, *Strong specialisation* captures whether an investor is more specialised in a portfolio company's industry than its immediate peers, whereas *Moderate specialisation* only requires an investor to be more specialised in that industry than the average investor in the VC market. Our analyses shown in Table 21 reveal that only *Strong specialisation* is detrimental to VC investors' value-added, whereas *Moderate specialisation* does not have any significant effect on VC investors' value-added. The coefficient for *Strong specialisation* is negative at the 1% level in the first regression (Column 1) and negative at the 5% when additional controls are introduced for VC investors' *Portfolio concentration* (Column 2). In both cases, the effect is also economically sizeable at 12.9% and 11.8% lower turnover growth, respectively. The finding reveals that very strong specialisation harms the value-adding capabilities of VC investors. This finding is intriguing as it highlights that only strong relative specialisation (greater than that of peers) is detrimental to value-added and not moderate specialisation (specialisation relative to the average investor in the market) and that it is compatible with the conventional wisdom that VC investors tend to specialise. We will discuss the implications in further detail in the next section.

However, when turning to moderating effects related to companies' maturity (Table 22), we do not find significant effects for VC investors' specialisation on turnover growth. In all regressions across the board, the interaction terms for all combinations of *Specialisation, Portfolio concentration, Strong specialisation* with both *Age* and *Round number* are insignificant (Table 22, Columns 1–6). Hence, our finding suggests that, within our sample of young high-growth companies, the effects of specialisation on investor value-added are consistent across companies' development stages and we find no supporting evidence for Hypotheses 3 a and 3 b.

Table 21: GMM-SYS regressions of turnover growth with decomposition of specialisation metric

Variable	(1) GMM-SYS	(2) GMM-SYS
Strong specialisation	-0.129***	-0.118**
	(-2.685)	(-2.540)
Moderate specialisation	-0.0419	-0.00596
	(-0.488)	(-0.0764)
Portfolio concentration		-0.0968**
		(-2.100)
ln(Past deals)	-0.0188	-0.0289
	(-0.953)	(-1.518)
Syndicate dummy	-0.0466	-0.00287
	(-0.884)	(-0.0524)
l.ln(Turnover)	-0.195***	-0.183***
	(-6.208)	(-6.278)
Age	0.0111	0.00811
	(1.363)	(1.061)
Round number	0.0182	0.0325*
	(0.874)	(1.831)
Constant	1.631***	1.583***
	(10.81)	(11.39)
Country FE	YES	YES
Industry FE	YES	YES
Year FE	YES	YES
AR1 p-value	0	0
AR2 p-value	0.00892	0.00859
AR3 p-value	0.846	0.815
Hansen J-statistic p-value	0.297	0.452
N	8,308	8,308

Table 21 shows GMM-SYS regressions (two-step system generalised method of moments estimator) with finite-sample correction of start-up turnover growth. *Strong specialisation* is a dummy variable equal to 1 if the modified *ICA* (average modified *ICA*) of an investor (investor syndicate) in a given year is >1 and is otherwise 0. *Moderate specialisation* is equal to 1 if the *ICA* (average *ICA*) of an investor (investor syndicate) in a given year is >1 but the modified *ICA* is <1. *Portfolio concentration* is a dummy variable equal to 1 if the *HHI* (average *HHI*) of an investor (investor syndicate) exceeds the median *HHI* value in our sample. Further details and the definitions of the remaining variables are presented in Section 4.3. Robust z-statistics are reported in parentheses. *, ** and *** denote statistical significance at the 10%, 5% and 1% level, respectively.

Table 22: GMM-SYS regressions of turnover growth with interaction effects

Variable	(1) GMM-SYS	(2) GMM-SYS	(3) GMM-SYS	(4) GMM-SYS	(5) GMM-SYS	(6) GMM-SYS
Specialisation	-0.0416			-0.122*		
	(-0.366)			(-1.755)		
Specialisation#Age	-0.00206					
	(-0.173)					
Portfolio concentration		-0.123			-0.0880	
		(-0.999)			(-1.130)	
Portfolio concentration#Age		0.000658				
		(0.0514)				
Strong specialisation			-0.0801			-0.150*
			(-0.666)			(-1.924)
Moderate specialisation			-0.0403			-0.00643
			(-0.530)			(-0.0745)
Strong specialisation#Age			-0.00114			
			(-0.0877)			
Specialisation#Round number				0.0140		
				(0.449)		
Portfolio concentration#RoundNr.					-0.0213	
					(-0.468)	
Strong specialisation#RoundNr.						0.0200
						(0.468)
Age	0.0139	0.0107	0.00933	-0.00593	0.00745	0.0106
	(1.350)	(1.025)	(0.790)	(-0.974)	(0.924)	(1.337)
ln(Past deals)	-0.0140	-0.0463***	-0.0170	-0.000500	-0.0358**	-0.0199
	(-0.729)	(-2.792)	(-0.883)	(-0.0285)	(-2.126)	(-1.044)
Syndicate dummy	-0.0603	0.0387	-0.0499	-0.0693	0.0152	-0.0525
	(-1.108)	(0.697)	(-0.935)	(-1.523)	(0.270)	(-1.015)
l.ln(Turnover)	-0.199***	-0.187***	-0.206***	-0.140***	-0.181***	-0.192***
	(-6.119)	(-5.974)	(-6.380)	(-6.278)	(-5.724)	(-6.496)
Round number	0.0193	0.0242	0.0266	0.0101	0.0276	0.0206
	(0.862)	(1.293)	(1.165)	(0.379)	(1.150)	(0.642)
Constant	1.595***	1.608***	1.691***	1.331***	1.561***	1.600***
	(10.14)	(11.23)	(10.15)	(11.94)	(10.46)	(11.31)

Variable	(1) GMM-SYS	(2) GMM-SYS	(3) GMM-SYS	(4) GMM-SYS	(5) GMM-SYS	(6) GMM-SYS
Country FE	YES	YES	YES	YES	YES	YES
Industry FE	YES	YES	YES	YES	YES	YES
Year FE	YES	YES	YES	YES	YES	YES
AR1 p-value	0	0	0	0	0	0
AR2 p-value	0.00806	0.00730	0.00868	0.00748	0.00709	0.00882
AR3 p-value	0.800	0.734	0.808	0.847	0.738	0.835
Hansen J-statistic p-value	0.233	0.285	0.441	0.981	0.175	0.397
N	8,308	8,308	8,308	8,308	8,308	8,308

Table 22 shows GMM-SYS regressions (two-step system generalised method of moments estimator) with finite-sample correction of start-up turnover growth. *Specialisation* is a dummy variable equal to 1 if the *ICA* (average *ICA*) of an investor (investor syndicate) in a given year is >1 and is otherwise 0. *Moderate specialisation* is equal to 1 if the *ICA* (average *ICA*) of an investor (investor syndicate) in a given year is >1 but the modified *ICA* is <1. *Portfolio concentration* is a dummy variable equal to 1 if the *HHI* (average *HHI*) of an investor (investor syndicate) exceeds the median *HHI* value in our sample. Further details and the definitions of the remaining variables are presented in Section 4.3. Robust z-statistics are reported in parentheses. *, ** and *** denote statistical significance at the 10%, 5% and 1% level, respectively.

4.4.3 Further Analyses and Robustness Checks

In order to ensure the robustness of our findings, we conduct a series of additional tests. First, and foremost, we add additional controls for the presence of different investor types. Certain investor types, such as governmental, bank or corporate venture capitalists (GVC, BVC, CVC), have been found to differ from IVCs in their ability to add value to companies (Chemmanur et al., 2014; Grilli and Murtinu, 2014; Cumming and Murtinu, 2016; Colombo and Murtinu, 2017). As the degree of specialisation of these investors may differ from independent investors, we undertake a robustness check to rule out the possibility that these investor characteristics, which have not hitherto been accounted for, drive the results. Specifically, we add additional control variables for the presence of a GVC, BVC, CVC, university VC (UVC), BA or any other non-IVC type of investors in the last financing round. The results of these analyses are presented in Table 23.

The results for *Strong specialisation* in our full regression specification (Table 23, Column 5) are virtually unchanged relative to our main findings (compare Table 21, Column 2): the coefficient for *Strong specialisation* changes from -0.118 to -0.119, and that of the corresponding t-statistic from -2.540 to -2.548 (which results in an increase in significance to the 1% level) while the coefficient for *Portfolio concentration* changes only at the third decimal place (from -0.0968 to -0.0911) accompanied by a slight decrease in its t-statistic (from -2.100 to -2.005). Besides that, our other findings also remain highly robust to this test, with only minor decreases in co-efficient size or significance. However, several of the different investor type dummies show significant coefficients, which underscores the fact that investor types differ in their ability to add value and highlights the importance of our test.

Table 23: GMM-SYS regressions accounting for presence of different investor types

Variable	(1) GMM-SYS	(2) GMM-SYS	(3) GMM-SYS	(4) GMM-SYS	(5) GMM-SYS
Specialisation	-0.0752*		-0.0740		
	(-1.670)		(-1.643)		
Portfolio concentration		-0.105**	-0.113**		-0.0911**
		(-2.238)	(-2.525)		(-2.005)
Strong specialisation				-0.116**	-0.119***
				(-2.403)	(-2.584)
Moderate specialisation				0.0473	0.0426
				(0.589)	(0.552)
CVC	0.0993	0.127*	0.132*	0.129*	0.157**
	(1.478)	(1.790)	(1.916)	(1.835)	(2.240)
BVC	0.0367	0.0545	0.0466	0.0531	0.0566
	(0.674)	(1.008)	(0.887)	(0.982)	(1.093)
GVC	-0.0509	-0.0200	-0.0465	-0.0436	-0.0394
	(-0.903)	(-0.347)	(-0.835)	(-0.756)	(-0.696)
BA	-0.200***	-0.148**	-0.169**	-0.191***	-0.165**
	(-2.859)	(-1.992)	(-2.231)	(-2.618)	(-2.303)
OtherVC	-0.291	-0.217	-0.259	-0.339**	-0.285*
	(-1.416)	(-1.455)	(-1.561)	(-2.040)	(-1.693)
UVC	-0.410**	-0.378**	-0.380**	-0.407**	-0.373**
	(-2.414)	(-2.171)	(-2.090)	(-2.090)	(-1.974)
ln(Past deals)	-0.0152	-0.0414**	-0.0230	-0.0205	-0.0256
	(-0.831)	(-2.494)	(-1.276)	(-1.124)	(-1.436)
Syndicate dummy	-0.00420	0.0490	0.0425	0.00370	0.0430
	(-0.0798)	(0.879)	(0.778)	(0.0695)	(0.783)
l.ln(Turnover)	-0.168***	-0.172***	-0.162***	-0.179***	-0.171***
	(-7.213)	(-7.244)	(-7.238)	(-7.887)	(-7.845)
Age	0.00194	0.00493	0.00127	0.00418	0.00235
	(0.302)	(0.763)	(0.205)	(0.655)	(0.387)
Round number	0.000824	0.0140	0.0168	0.00698	0.0215
	(0.0377)	(0.707)	(0.873)	(0.317)	(1.107)

Variable	(1) GMM-SYS	(2) GMM-SYS	(3) GMM-SYS	(4) GMM-SYS	(5) GMM-SYS
Constant	1.494***	1.517***	1.464***	1.551***	1.505***
	(12.39)	(13.02)	(13.16)	(13.34)	(13.71)
Country FE	YES	YES	YES	YES	YES
Industry FE	YES	YES	YES	YES	YES
Year FE	YES	YES	YES	YES	YES
AR1 p-value	0	0	0	0	0
AR2 p-value	0.00769	0.00732	0.00772	0.00896	0.00880
AR3 p-value	0.858	0.773	0.822	0.876	0.850
Hansen J-statistic p-value	0.448	0.510	0.465	0.498	0.574
N	8,308	8,308	8,308	8,308	8,308

Table 23 shows GMM-SYS regressions (two-step system generalised method of moments estimator) with finite-sample correction of start-up turnover growth. *Specialisation* is a dummy variable equal to 1 if the *ICA* (average *ICA*) of an investor (investor syndicate) in a given year is >1 and is otherwise 0. *Strong specialisation* is a dummy variable equal to 1 if the modified *ICA* (average modified *ICA*) of an investor (investor syndicate) in a given year is >1 and is otherwise 0. *Moderate specialisation* is equal to 1 if the ICA (average *ICA*) of an investor (investor syndicate) in a given year is >1 but the modified *ICA* is <1. *Portfolio concentration* is a dummy variable equal to 1 if the *HHI* (average *HHI*) of an investor (investor syndicate) exceeds the median *HHI* value in our sample. *CVC, BVC, GVC, UVC, OtherVC* and *BA* are dummy variables that control for the presence of corporate, bank, governmental, university or other VC investors as well as business angels in the previous funding round, respectively. Further details and the definitions of the remaining variables are presented in Section 4.3. Robust z-statistics are reported in parentheses. *, ** and *** denote statistical significance at the 10%, 5% and 1% level, respectively.

As a second robustness check, we address the financial value-added of VC investors and add the natural logarithm of the amount of funding that a company raised in its last round of financing (*ln(Amount last round)*) as an additional control. This check is required as it is possible that specialist and generalist investors might differ in terms of their financial value-added (i.e. one of the two groups might contribute more financial means than the other). The results of this test are shown in Table 24.

Table 24: GMM-SYS regressions accounting for financial value-added

Variable	(1) GMM-SYS	(2) GMM-SYS	(3) GMM-SYS	(4) GMM-SYS	(5) GMM-SYS
Specialisation	-0.0961*		-0.0977*		
	(-1.848)		(-1.944)		
Portfolio concentration		-0.219***	-0.190***		-0.145**
		(-2.941)	(-2.737)		(-2.215)
Strong specialisation				-0.123**	-0.122**
				(-2.372)	(-2.470)
Moderate specialisation				-0.0229	-0.0168
				(-0.264)	(-0.210)
ln(Amount last round)	1.51e-05	2.16e-05	1.68e-05	1.61e-05	1.50e-05
	(0.719)	(1.001)	(0.833)	(0.786)	(0.781)
ln(Past deals)	-0.0516*	-0.107***	-0.0807**	-0.0604**	-0.0725**
	(-1.668)	(-2.885)	(-2.253)	(-1.998)	(-2.150)
Syndicate dummy	-0.0612	0.0232	0.00534	-0.0562	-0.00422
	(-0.908)	(0.319)	(0.0745)	(-0.859)	(-0.0627)
l.ln(Turnover)	-0.196***	-0.199***	-0.190***	-0.208***	-0.197***
	(-5.709)	(-6.078)	(-6.293)	(-6.365)	(-6.759)
Age	0.0123	0.0118	0.00940	0.0139*	0.0110
	(1.450)	(1.426)	(1.210)	(1.698)	(1.438)
Round number	-0.0123	0.00123	0.00805	-0.00227	0.0185
	(-0.500)	(0.0605)	(0.418)	(-0.0955)	(0.996)
Constant	1.787***	1.976***	1.882***	1.888***	1.875***
	(8.202)	(8.329)	(8.566)	(9.026)	(8.946)
Country FE	YES	YES	YES	YES	YES

108

Variable	(1) GMM-SYS	(2) GMM-SYS	(3) GMM-SYS	(4) GMM-SYS	(5) GMM-SYS
Industry FE	YES	YES	YES	YES	YES
Year FE	YES	YES	YES	YES	YES
AR1 p-value	0	0	0	0	0
AR2 p-value	0.0781	0.0729	0.0792	0.0832	0.0813
AR3 p-value	0.444	0.483	0.435	0.429	0.424
Hansen J-statistic p-value	0.370	0.510	0.519	0.419	0.609
N	6,751	6,751	6,751	6,751	6,751

Table 24 shows GMM-SYS regressions (two-step system generalised method of moments estimator) with finite-sample correction of start-up turnover growth. *Specialisation* is a dummy variable equal to 1 if the *ICA* (average *ICA*) of an investor (investor syndicate) in a given year is >1 and is otherwise 0. *Strong specialisation* is a dummy variable equal to 1 if the modified *ICA* (average modified *ICA*) of an investor (investor syndicate) in a given year is >1 and is otherwise 0. *Moderate specialisation* is equal to 1 if the *ICA* (average *ICA*) of an investor (investor syndicate) in a given year is >1 but the modified *ICA* is <1. *Portfolio concentration* is a dummy variable equal to 1 if the *HHI* (average *HHI*) of an investor (investor syndicate) exceeds the median *HHI* value in our sample. *Ln(Amount last round)* is the natural logarithm of the amount of funding raised in the previous funding round. Further details and the definitions of the remaining variables are presented in Section 4.3. Robust z-statistics are reported in parentheses. *, ** and *** denote statistical significance at the 10%, 5% and 1% level, respectively.

Although the sample size decreases by about 20% as a result of the funding amount not being available for all financing rounds in our sample, the results for our independent variables are again very similar in terms of significance. In terms of magnitude, the coefficients for *Specialisation, Strong specialisation* and *Moderate specialisation* are, in most cases, extremely similar to those of our main analyses, while the size of the coefficient for *Portfolio concentration* even increases across all regressions. Thus, we conclude that the lower value-added of specialised investors is not driven by differences in financial value-added (i.e. the amount of funding provided by these investors).

Third, we add control variables for the average levels of specialisation and portfolio concentration of those investors which were active in the focal company's home country at the respective point in time. In doing so, we address the concern that the level of specialisation may differ across countries due to differences in the institutional setting and the local VC market whilst also addressing the concern that certain countries may be overrepresented in the sample. However, our results (shown in Table 25) are virtually unaffected by this change.

Finally, as mentioned in Section 4.3.3, we need to be careful how we measure specialisation and investor–company-fit for syndicates. Our default approach is to use the average, value-weighted, *ICA* and *HHI* to determine *Specialisation* and *Portfolio concentration* (see Section 4.3.3. for details). By using the average for syndicates, the calculation implicitly weighs investor influence in a syndicate in a manner that is commensurate with their degree of specialisation – hence, it is possible that investors with very high (or low) values of *ICA* or *HHI* disproportionately affect the syndication metric for the syndicate. In order to test the robustness of our findings, we do not use the value-weighted average *ICA* of a syndicate for determining the overall syndicate specialisation but, instead, employ the share of specialised investors in a syndicate as a metric.[22] The results (shown in Table 26) are highly robust to this fundamental change in measuring our specialisation variable.

Table 25: GMM-SYS regressions accounting for potential differences in specialisation practices at the country-level

Variable	(1) GMM-SYS	(2) GMM-SYS	(3) GMM-SYS	(4) GMM-SYS	(5) GMM-SYS
Specialisation	-0.113**		-0.0960**		
	(-2.279)		(-2.043)		
Portfolio concentration		-0.131**	-0.119**		-0.0896*
		(-2.526)	(-2.468)		(-1.901)
Strong specialisation				-0.131***	-0.117**
				(-2.688)	(-2.508)
Moderate specialisation				-0.0452	-0.000266
				(-0.522)	(-0.00335)
Country avg. Specialisation	-0.0113		0.00509	-0.0189	-0.0287
	(-0.0860)		(0.0399)	(-0.142)	(-0.224)
Country avg. Portfolio concentration		-0.0253	-0.0359		-0.0274
		(-0.227)	(-0.326)		(-0.251)
ln(Past deals)	-0.0139	-0.0436**	-0.0275	-0.0193	-0.0285
	(-0.706)	(-2.466)	(-1.394)	(-0.979)	(-1.490)
Syndicate dummy	-0.0463	0.0319	0.00877	-0.0452	-0.00446
	(-0.877)	(0.552)	(0.158)	(-0.859)	(-0.0814)
l.ln(Turnover)	-0.186***	-0.189***	-0.178***	-0.194***	-0.183***

---

22 For example, consider an investment round with three investors of which two have an *ICA* greater than 1 and one investor has an *ICA* smaller than 1. In this case, the share of specialised investors (*Specialist share*) is 0.66.

Variable	(1) GMM-SYS	(2) GMM-SYS	(3) GMM-SYS	(4) GMM-SYS	(5) GMM-SYS
	(-5.848)	(-5.955)	(-6.126)	(-6.202)	(-6.301)
Age	0.00913	0.0109	0.00765	0.0110	0.00824
	(1.111)	(1.340)	(1.008)	(1.350)	(1.077)
Round number	0.0108	0.0245	0.0268	0.0180	0.0318*
	(0.504)	(1.283)	(1.474)	(0.868)	(1.778)
Constant	1.580***	1.621***	1.567***	1.639***	1.609***
	(8.580)	(10.03)	(8.743)	(9.227)	(9.050)
Country FE	YES	YES	YES	YES	YES
Industry FE	YES	YES	YES	YES	YES
Year FE	YES	YES	YES	YES	YES
AR1 p-value	0	0	0	0	0
AR2 p-value	0.00820	0.00733	0.00808	0.00886	0.00864
AR3 p-value	0.843	0.728	0.801	0.849	0.819
Hansen J-statistic p-value	0.239	0.228	0.311	0.299	0.440
N	8,308	8,308	8,308	8,308	8,308

Table 25 shows GMM-SYS regressions (two-step system generalised method of moments estimator) with finite-sample correction of start-up turnover growth. *Specialisation* is a dummy variable equal to 1 if the *ICA* (average *ICA*) of an investor (investor syndicate) in a given year is >1 and is otherwise 0. *Strong specialisation* is a dummy variable equal to 1 if the modified *ICA* (average modified *ICA*) of an investor (investor syndicate) in a given year is >1 and is otherwise 0. *Moderate specialisation* is equal to 1 if the *ICA* (average *ICA*) of an investor (investor syndicate) in a given year is >1 but the modified *ICA* is <1. *Portfolio concentration* is a dummy variable equal to 1 if the *HHI* (average *HHI*) of an investor (investor syndicate) exceeds the median *HHI* value in our sample. *Country avg. Specialisation* and *Country avg. Portfolio concentration* are the averages of *Specialisation* and *Portfolio concentration* of investors who are active in the respective portfolio companies' country at a given point in time. Further details and the definitions of the remaining variables are presented in Section 4.3. Robust z-statistics are reported in parentheses. *, ** and *** denote statistical significance at the 10%, 5% and 1% level, respectively.

Table 26: GMM-SYS regressions with alternative specialisation metric calculation in syndicates

Variable	(1) GMM-SYS	(2) GMM-SYS	(3) GMM-SYS	(4) GMM-SYS	(5) GMM-SYS
Specialist share	-0.0979*		-0.0829*		
	(-1.847)		(-1.649)		
Concentrated investor share		-0.101**	-0.0861*		-0.0554
		(-2.014)	(-1.745)		(-1.121)
Strong specialist share				-0.139***	-0.119**
				(-2.723)	(-2.456)
Moderate specialist share				-0.0268	0.00762
				(-0.264)	(0.0802)
l.ln(Turnover)	-0.178***	-0.187***	-0.166***	-0.184***	-0.165***
	(-5.573)	(-5.853)	(-5.490)	(-5.763)	(-5.501)
Age	0.00764	0.0112	0.00604	0.00853	0.00484
	(0.924)	(1.327)	(0.752)	(1.028)	(0.607)
Round number	0.00304	0.0187	0.0152	0.00921	0.0152
	(0.143)	(0.939)	(0.828)	(0.442)	(0.830)
ln(Past deals)	-0.0155	-0.0407**	-0.0267	-0.0203	-0.0286
	(-0.772)	(-2.413)	(-1.372)	(-0.987)	(-1.479)
Syndicate dummy	-0.0430	0.00805	-0.0114	-0.0294	-0.00788
	(-0.783)	(0.150)	(-0.213)	(-0.535)	(-0.149)
Constant	1.531***	1.583***	1.468***	1.585***	1.480***
	(9.904)	(10.56)	(10.34)	(10.29)	(10.41)
Country FE	YES	YES	YES	YES	YES
Industry FE	YES	YES	YES	YES	YES
Year FE	YES	YES	YES	YES	YES
AR1 p-value	0	0	0	0	0
AR2 p-value	0.00761	0.00742	0.00750	0.00862	0.00827
AR3 p-value	0.807	0.750	0.793	0.832	0.823

Variable	(1) GMM-SYS	(2) GMM-SYS	(3) GMM-SYS	(4) GMM-SYS	(5) GMM-SYS
Hansen J-statistic p-value	0.122	0.215	0.163	0.114	0.262
N	8,308	8,308	8,308	8,308	8,308

Table 26 shows GMM-SYS regressions (two-step system generalised method of moments estimator) with finite-sample correction of start-up turnover growth. *Specialist share* is the share of investors present in a given round whose *ICA* is greater than 1. *Concentrated inv share* is the share of investors present in a given round whose *HHI* is greater than the median *HHI* value in our sample. *Strong specialist share* is the share of investors present in a given round whose *modified ICA* is greater than 1 and *Moderate specialist share* is the share of investors present in a given round whose *ICA* is greater than 1 but whose *modified ICA* is smaller than 1. Further details and the definitions of the remaining variables are presented in Sections 4.3 and 4.4.3. Robust z-statistics are reported in parentheses. *, ** and *** denote statistical significance at the 10%, 5% and 1% level, respectively.

4.5 Discussion

The relationship between VC investors and their portfolio companies remains one of the most interesting, yet complex areas of entrepreneurship research. With our analyses, we aim at deepening the understanding of the ways in which investors create value for portfolio companies and how their specialisation strategy affects their ability to select promising ventures. Our findings offer several contributions to the extant literature on VC investors' selection and value-added (e.g., Chemmanur et al., 2011; Croce et al., 2013), diversification vs. specialisation as a VC strategy (Gompers et al., 2009; Buchner et al., 2017) as well as organisational learning (Matusik and Fitza, 2012).

First, we find that industry specialisation negatively affects VC investors' value-added. This effect is consistent across the development stages of ventures. Moreover, the negative effect of high venture capitalist specialisation on performance of a venture occurs even when the investor–company-fit is high (i.e. when a portfolio company operates in the field of expertise of a specialised investor), suggesting that the disadvantages from greater specialisation (i.e. the absence of diverse experience) clearly outweigh the benefits (i.e. greater industry and domain expertise). In that regard, our results are in line with prior research which found diversified VC funds to be more successful (Knill, 2009; Humphery-Jenner, 2013; Buchner et al., 2017) and which support the notion that the diverse knowledge stock of non-specialised VC investors is a valuable resource for ventures (Matusik and Fitza, 2012), as it may equip investors with superior problem-solving skills (Ahuja and Katila, 2001), foster analogical thinking (Gavetti et al., 2005) and allows investors to advise companies on the multiple possible trajectories (Matusik and Fitza, 2012). In that regard, our findings contrast with those from the research by Cressy et al. (2007), who investigate a similar question in the context of private equity buyouts in the UK and employ a similar explanatory variable. However, Cressy et al. (2007) find that specialisation confers a competitive advantage for private equity investors in buyout transactions, as industry specialisation leads to superior post-buyout operating performance for the acquired companies. We thus conclude that early-stage investors require a different set of capabilities in order to add value to companies and that these capabilities are better acquired through diverse experience than through deep industry knowledge.

Moreover, our findings reveal that the effect is driven by VC investors with particularly high levels of specialisation, exceeding those of their peers. This finding has three implications: first, it hints at a non-linear relationship between investor specialisation and value-added, which has also been discussed by Matusik and Fitza (2012). Second, it underscores that moderate levels of specialisation (defined as specialisation relative to the market but not relative to peer investors active in the focal industry) do not negatively affect investor value-added, which is an important observation given that many VC investors tend to specialise. Put differently, investors should maintain a sufficient level of diversification and should avoid specialising more strongly than their immediate peers in order to avoid the scenario where their value-adding capabilities are negatively affected. Third, it suggests that the degree of specialisation can indeed be a source of competitive advantage, as argued by Cressy et al. (2007). However, the optimal levels of specialisation seem to differ for VC and private equity investors, as the comparison of our results with those of Cressy et al. (2007) implies.

In addition, the fact that both a narrow investment focus (as reflected by high *Portfolio concentration*) and high degrees of investor–company-fit (as reflected by *Specialisation*) have a *distinct* impact on the value-added by investors suggests that specialised knowledge stock is not only a disadvantage for investors, but also that high levels of investor–company-fit can be detrimental to investor value-added. While prior research (Lungeanu and Zajac, 2016) has typically discussed the notion of investor–company-fit as a positive feature that increases the relevance of an investor's knowledge base, our findings suggest that a greater investor–company-fit might have negative effects. More specifically, we argue that it increases the risk of knowledge appropriation or information leakage to competitors of the ventures in a VC investor's portfolio (Ueda, 2004; Pahnke et al., 2015), thus impairing investor value-added. The negative effects can be caused directly or the risk of knowledge appropriation and information leakage could induce ventures to set up defensive strategies which, in turn, harms the working relationship between them and the VC investors and is detrimental to investor value-added.

Nonetheless, when specialisation is paired with high investor–company-fit, specialised investors show superior selection capabilities that offset their inferior value-added. This fact is reflected in differences in our results between the OLS and GMM-SYS regressions. Even though specialised investors add less value to ventures (as evidenced by the GMM regressions), these ventures do not show any differences in growth according to the OLS regressions, which implies that VC investors have selected ventures with greater intrinsic growth potential. Hence, the findings provide evidence in favour of the argument that VC investors benefit from a specialised investment strategy, as their greater industry knowledge reduces critical information asymmetries and seems to equip them with superior investment selection skills. This is in line with the arguments presented by Gompers et al. (2009). Hence, this essay is one of the first to reveal heterogeneity among VC investors in their ability to select ventures with greater inherent growth potential, whilst accounting for endogeneity (i.e. we are able to provide empirical evidence revealing that some VC investors are better than others in selecting high-potential companies). Our study further highlights that specialisation may have opposing effects on investors' ability to select and add value to ventures, which makes it particularly interesting to investigate how investors deal with this trade-off. Consequently, our research also contributes to the stream on VC selection and VC decision-making processes (Kirsch et al., 2009; Petty and Gruber, 2011). Finally, it is worth noting that selection by specialist VC investors and inferior value-adding capabilities may be related to one another. It is possible that differences in the resource allocation between scouting and coaching for specialised and non-specialised investors may otherwise explain the results. For example, it is possible that specialised investors focus on the selection of deals as opposed to portfolio work.

Our findings on the inferior value-added of specialised investors are robust to several alternative specifications in terms of the measurement of specialisation, and it is important to stress that the results have significant explanatory power. As a consequence, our results call for further investigation into whether differences in VC investor specialisation may help explain some of the performance and value-adding heterogeneity among different investor types (e.g., Chemmanur et al., 2014; Grilli and Murtinu, 2014; Cumming and Murtinu, 2016; Colombo and Murtinu, 2017).

In practice, our research informs both entrepreneurs and VC investors. First, start-ups should source funding from diversified investors, where possible, in order to draw most value from the investor–investee relationship. However, VC investors need to identify and manage an optimal level of specialisation, as the results of this research suggest that venture capitalists face a trade-off between acquiring strong industry specialisation, which helps them select high-potential companies, and diverse experience, which is beneficial for their value-add. Moreover, VC investors can act on our findings by forming syndicates in which specialised VC investors focus on selection while non-specialised investors focus on the operational value-added, as this would allow VC investors to potentially get the 'best of both worlds' through the effective allocation of their skills.

Our research has certain limitations which offer several avenues for future research. First, we consider each VC investor as a monolithic bloc, and are unable to evaluate the differences in the value-adding capabilities among investment managers within one VC firm. This extension of our analysis would be worthwhile, as VC investment managers have different investment styles which also shape the trajectory of the ventures they invest in (e.g., Gompers et al., 2009; Ewens and Rhodes-Kropf, 2015). Moreover, it would be interesting to assess the effect that VC investor specialisation has on their value-added in terms of innovation (patenting), where one would intuitively expect the positive effects of greater domain expertise. Existing research notes negative effects on ventures which are linked to competitors via their VC investors (Pahnke et al., 2015). Finally, it would be worthwhile to assess the effect of specialised expertise as an antecedent for VC investors' syndication behaviour.

4.6 Conclusion

In this essay, we use the VICO 4.0 dataset, sponsored by the European Commission, to analyse 8,308 company-year observations from European and Israeli start-up companies and the related investor information. We do this in order to evaluate how VC investors' industry specialisation and investor–company-fit drive VC investors' value-added and their ability to select ventures with greater inherent potential. We find that industry specialisation paired with appropriate investor–company-fit allows VC investors to 'pick' ventures with superior intrinsic growth prospects, suggesting that a deeper understanding of industry dynamics reduces critical information asymmetries. This study is one of the first to empirically unveil and explain heterogeneity among VC investors in their ability to select ventures with greater inherent development potential. However, our findings also suggest VC investors' narrow expertise and strong specialisation hamper their ability to add value to portfolio companies – even in circumstances where the investor–company-fit is high (i.e. if these ventures operate within investors' area of expertise). Our findings suggest that early-stage investors benefit from acquiring a diverse knowledge stock rather than specialised industry expertise. Additionally, our results provide evidence supporting the view that greater investor–company-fit may impair investor value-added due to knowledge appropriation effects or information leakage to competitors. Our results are robust to multiple alternative regression specifications. Consequently, we also contribute to the literature on investor value-added by providing novel empirical evidence that sheds light on the question of *how* investors add value to companies while highlighting industry experience as an antecedent for investor value-added.

5 How the Investor–Company-Fit Shapes VC Syndication in Europe

The essay presented in this chapter links industry specialisation and investor–company-fit with VC investors' selection capabilities and their deal-structuring practices to provide an integrated perspective on the operational consequences of VC investors' specialisation strategy. Thereby, this chapters answers Research Question 3. The chapter is structured as follows: The first section, 5.1, reviews the literature and Section 5.2 derives the hypotheses. Section 5.3. elaborates on the dataset, variables, sample construction and method. Section 5.4 presents the empirical analyses and results. Section 5.5 presents a discussion of the results and the limitations of this research. Finally, Section 5.6 presents concluding remarks.[23,24]

5.1 Literature Review

In the VC industry, investors often do not invest alone, but syndicate the funding of companies such that several investors provide financing for a venture in a given investment round (Ferrary, 2010). The widespread cooperation of VC investors is a distinct characteristic of the VC industry (Jääskeläinen, 2012). In practice, around half of VC investments in Europe are syndicated, whereas syndication is more common in the US (Wright and Lockett, 2003; Jääskeläinen et al., 2006; Manigart et al., 2006).

We structure the literature on syndication into three categories, which are derived from the syndication process: the decision and motivation to

---

23 This chapter is largely based on a joint working paper with Professor Carolin Bock (Technische Universität Darmstadt) and Professor Massimiliano Guerini (Politecnico di Milano) and it is thus written from the first-person-plural point of view (i.e., *we*) to indicate that the research also reflects the opinions of the co-authors. A version of the working paper titled 'How investor-company-fit shapes venture capital syndication in Europe' was presented at the Fourth Entrepreneurial Finance Conference (ENTFIN) in Trier, Germany, in July 2019.

24 The working paper that forms the basis of this chapter received support from the 'RISIS Research infrastructures for the assessment of science, technology and innovation policy' project, funded by the European Union under the Seventh Framework Program (Grant Agreement n°313082).

syndicate; the composition and dynamics of syndicates; and the outcomes of syndication (i.e. the effects of syndication on investors' and portfolio companies' performance) (Jääskeläinen, 2012). After reviewing the broader themes in terms of outcomes as well as composition and dynamics of syndicates, we turn to a detailed review of the literature on investors' decisions and motivations to syndicate, specifically emphasising prior literature that has examined the links between specialised expertise and syndication.

Regarding outcomes, researchers including Brander et el. (2002), Tian (2012) and Das et al. (2011) evaluate the effects of syndication on deal selection and value-added. Das et al. (2011) find that syndication may improve deal selection as well as investor value-adding, where the latter is reflected in the likelihood of and time to exit. Similarly, Tian (2012) reports that syndicates create additional value for ventures as syndicate-backed companies have higher chances of achieving a successful exit and reach higher IPO market valuations. Brander et al. (2002) find that syndicated investments have higher returns than sole investments and conclude that the higher returns are caused by greater investor value-added in syndicated investments.

When it comes to the composition and dynamics of syndicates, recent research has been devoted to the choice of syndicate partners, the formation of syndicate networks, and their relationship with investors' status and reputation (e.g., Milanov and Shepherd, 2013; Hopp and Lukas, 2014; Hochberg et al., 2015; Gompers et al., 2016b). Milanov and Shepherd (2013) analyse how newcomers' initial syndication network affects their subsequent network formation and reputation. The authors find that the reputation of newcomers' first partners has an ongoing positive influence on their future status, even when controlling for other, intermediate affiliations, which underscores the importance of syndicate relationships for VC investors. Hopp and Lukas (2014) analyse how VC investors choose syndicate partners in the German market, by analysing which characteristics affect the partnering decision. The results suggest that a complex construct of time-variant signals related to experience and reciprocity shapes investors' partner choice. Hochberg et al. (2015) investigate how ties between different VC investors are formed and provide evidence that investors form syndicates in order to accumulate additional resources. Interestingly, the results suggest that investors trade resources when forming syndicates: for instance, investors seem to trade capital for experience and deal access. However, while the work of Hochberg et al. (2015) significantly advances the understanding of how the dynamics of syndicate networks unfold, it does not touch on the question why certain deals are syndicated and others not. In another paper on the matter at hand, Gompers et al. (2016 b) analyse the choice of syndicate partners on a personal level. The authors find that investors who share personal characteristics such as ethnicity, education or career backgrounds have a higher likelihood of forming syndicates with one another. However, the documented homophily negatively affects outcomes, as it lowers the likelihood of investment success by more than 20%, suggesting that syndicates formed by high-affinity investors make inferior decisions.

Regarding the decision and motives to syndicate, extant research has identified a handful of categories that classify investors' motives to syndicate. Building on the very similar categorisations by Manigart et al. (2006), Manigart and Wright (2013), Lockett and Wright (2001) and Jääskeläinen (2012), we group the motives into four main categories. The first two motivational drivers are linked to investors' portfolio management, whereas the latter two are deal-specific.

Risk sharing ('portfolio diversification'): While the investments of VC investors are inherently risky, the risk, as in any other investment, comes in two variants: systematic and idiosyncratic risk (Lockett and Wright, 2001). According to classical finance theory (Markowitz, 1952), the latter kind of risk can be addressed through diversification. However, the size of VC funds is a limiting factor for attaining a fully diversified portfolio (Sahlman, 1990). Syndication by VC investors can thus be seen as a response to this fact, as it allows investors to spread their investments across a greater number of portfolio companies at lower transaction costs (Kaiser and Lauterbach, 2007), which allows them to reduce portfolio risk without affecting expected returns (Wang and Wang, 2012).

Deal-flow generation: The identification of and the access to investment opportunities, via deal flow, is vital to VC firms' success (Manigart and Wright, 2013). By sharing investment opportunities through syndication, a VC firm may create an expectation for future reciprocation that in turn allows it to gain access to further promising deals (Manigart et al., 2006; Hopp and Lukas, 2013).

Deal selection ('ex-ante risk reduction') is the first deal-specific motive: VCs' investments in portfolio companies are inherently risky due to information asymmetries between investors and entrepreneurs, and syndication may improve investment selection through collaboration of investors in evaluating risky deals (Lerner, 1994; Brander et al., 2002). For instance, it has been argued that the lead investor initiates the formation of a syndicate if the venture capitalist's own evaluation of the investment opportunity is insufficient to come up with a clear decision whether or not to pursue the investment, and the investor thus prefers to get a second opinion by another venture capitalist (Lerner, 1994; Brander et al., 2002).

Value-adding ('ex-post risk reduction') has been discussed as a second deal-specific motive. Syndication may improve VC firms' ability to manage their investments and create value for their portfolio companies, as the syndicate partners may provide additional specialist expertise, for instance in industries with which a VC firm is less familiar (Dimov and Milanov, 2010; Hopp, 2010).

However, although the general motivational drivers of syndication are theoretically well understood, extant research, which is typically survey-based (e.g., Lockett and Wright, 2001; Wright and Lockett, 2003; Manigart et al., 2006) falls short of providing a fine-grained understanding of the driving forces for investors' decision to share a *particular* investment opportunity with co-investors and to undertake others individually (Jääske-läinen, 2012). We want to address this shortage by analysing the role of industry specialisation and investor–company-fit for syndicate formation and partner choice. Not only is industry specialisation an important aspect of VC strategy (Gompers et al., 2009; Knill et al., 2009; Matusik and Fitza, 2012; Cressy et al., 2014), it seems also likely that the fit of specialised expertise is a factor affecting investors' deal-specific motive to syndicate for deal selection purposes. In short, we presume that the investor–company-fit is likely to affect the degree of information asymmetries that investors face and thus could be related to investors' *deal selection motive* (Manigart et al., 2006). But before deriving our hypotheses in detail, we briefly review the extant literature on industry specialisation and syndication to further highlight the need for the analysis we propose.

First of all, and closely related to our research, Manigart et al. (2006) conduct a survey on VC syndication in six European countries. They hypothesise that the industry specialisation of the investor is relevant for the selection motive, and argue that specialised investors have a deeper understanding of their industry and consequently face lower informational asymmetries when assessing investment options. However, the authors find only limited support for the notion that industry specialisation affects the selection motive. Specifically, their survey data suggests that the deal selection motive is significantly less important for VC firms that are specialised in a specific industry, but the finding only occurs in their subsample of early-stage investors. However, the authors acknowledge that '[the] lack of more significant findings should be treated with caution, however, as we rely upon a crude measure of VC firm specialisation. Research that uses a more refined measure of VC specialisation may yield stronger conclusions' (Manigart et al., 2006, p. 148).

Second, Hopp (2010) investigates a related research question, evaluating the effect of the absolute levels of industry experience as an antecedent for syndication. The author reports that VC investors with greater industry experience syndicate to a *greater* extent, which contradicts the finding of Manigart et al. (2006). However, Hopp (2010) relies on a very short-term-oriented and coarse measure for industry experience, namely the number of deals a VC investor conducted in a given industry in the previous year. Given that the investors in Hopp's (2010) sample on average only conduct 0.5 investments per year across different industries (i.e. one investment every second year), the employed measure for specialisation will fluctuate greatly over time and is thus not very well suited to track a VC investors' actual industry knowledge. Besides that, the generalizability of Hopp's (2010) findings is limited, as the analyses only cover German companies. Consequently, the differences with the findings of Manigart et al. (2006) could well be driven by methodological shortcomings, geographical differences, or the fact that Hopp (2010) uses secondary data (which is beneficial in this context (Jääskeläinen, 2012; De Clerq and Dimov, 2004)), whereas Manigart et al. (2006) essentially measured intended (rather than realised) behaviour based on a survey.

Third, De Clerq and Dimov (2004) use a measure for portfolio concentration (the Herfindahl-Hirschman-Index) as a proxy for investor specialisation to assess its effects on syndication at the VC firm portfolio level. The authors find only weak support for the hypothesis that greater specialised industry knowledge leads to a lower likelihood of syndication. However, as the authors use yearly aggregated data, they acknowledge that they may have 'overlooked important variation' (De Clerq and Dimov, 2004, p. 255).

In total, the review shows that the extant literature on VC syndication has accounted for VC specialisation only in a very limited manner and that the findings of extant research are contradictory and weak, which may well be driven by several shortcomings. First, the variables to measure specialisation are typically coarse (Manigart et al., 2006; Hopp, 2010). Second, the analyses are conducted at an aggregate level (i.e. by using investor-year observations rather than deal-level data), such that important variation is missing (De Clercq and Dimov, 2004). Third, in all the aforementioned papers, the definition of specialisation is problematic, as it neglects the *fit* between investors' specialised (industry) expertise and the needs of the portfolio company (i.e. its industry), which is an important factor in this context (Lungeanu and Zajac, 2016). Fourth, in the case of Manigart et al.

123

(2006), the nature of survey-based research implies that it is capturing intended rather than realised investment behaviour, which is unfavourable as it does not allow for the derivation of fine-grained insights on investors' actual decisions (De Clerq and Dimov, 2004; Jääskeläinen, 2012). In conclusion, the opportunity to overcome the shortcomings of prior research and to provide a more nuanced perspective on the matter warrants an empirical analysis of this topic.

5.2 Hypotheses Development

Syndicates are typically run and organised by a lead investor, who originates the financing round (Ferrary, 2010) and thus has the prerogative to invite other co-investors, which are typically less active (Lerner, 1994; De Clercq and Dimov, 2004; Manigart et al., 2006). However, syndication is costly, in particular for the lead investor, as the lead VC investor must share the deal proceeds with its co-investors if a syndicate is formed (Brander et al., 2002). Hence, the lead investor would only initiate the formation of a syndicate if it is advantageous and the benefits from syndication outweigh its cost (Brander et al., 2002).

When investing in companies, VC investors face significant information asymmetries between themselves and their (potential) investee companies, which cause severe information problems (Gompers et al., 1995; Amit et al., 1998). Consequently, investors may choose to syndicate in order to gather additional opinions on the investment opportunity and improve the screening, as syndication allows for the gathering of more information (Lerner, 1994; Brander et al., 2002; Casamatta and Haritchabalet, 2007). Consequently, if an investor faces less information asymmetries, the need to syndicate for screening purposes (i.e. the impact of the screening motive outlined above) will be lower. However, specialised expertise and greater investor–company-fit may effectively reduce information asymmetries for investors. For instance, Gompers et al. (2009) argue that specialised VC investors may become industry experts possessing a superior understanding of technology, markets and people, and that greater expertise would lead to better investments within an industry. Similarly, Manigart et al. (2006) argue that specialised investors have a deeper understanding of their industry and consequently face less information asymmetries. Building on these arguments, we consider industry specialisation and investor–company-fit to be functional antecedents for syndication, as they reduce information asymmetries and thus improve the accuracy and the outcomes of individual investments (Jääskälainen, 2012). As argued above, the reduced information asymmetries from greater industry specialisation and investor–company-fit would in turn reduce the need for lead investors to initiate the formation of a syndicate, as no additional screening resources are required. Commensurately, we formulate:

Hypothesis 1: The higher the fit between the specialised expertise of the lead investor and the focal venture, the less likely the lead investor is to syndicate the deal.

As outlined above, we hypothesise that both investor–company-fit and syndication are means to reduce investors' ex-ante risk through the reduction of information asymmetries. However, risk and information asymmetries vary across companies' development stage and are higher in the earlier stages of financing when companies are younger (Sapienza et al., 1996; Plummer et al., 2015), such that the impact of specialisation on the propensity to syndicate may vary across financing stages. Consequently, it is important to address potential moderating effects. This necessity is further underscored by the fact that the findings by Manigart et al. (2006) are only significant in a subsample of investors investing in early-stage companies. Unfortunately, however, Manigart et al. (2006) are not able to account for potential interaction effects due to their less granular survey data. Notwithstanding, their subsample results would be consistent with the explanation that alleged effect of investor–company-fit on VC syndication is greater in situations in which investors face greater risk and information asymmetries, as superior screening capabilities might be more valuable in these situations. Hence, we propose the following hypothesis:

Hypothesis 2: Venture age moderates the relationship between investor–company-fit and syndication, such that the younger the venture, the greater the negative effect of investor–company-fit on syndication.

When a lead investor decides to form a syndicate, the next important, and therefore closely related, step is to invite (i.e. choose) the co-investors (Lerner, 1994; De Clercq and Dimov, 2004; Manigart et al., 2006). Prior research has identified several factors that make VC investors attractive partners. For instance, Lockett and Wright (1999) highlight that (positive) past interactions with the potential partner are an important criterion for lead investors. Moreover, reputation (Lockett and Wright, 2001) and status (Lerner, 1994) are important factors that make syndicate partners more attractive. However, as outlined above, recent research from Hochberg et al. (2015) highlights that investors seek to augment the set of resources through syndication and actively trade complementary resources. In Hypo-thesis 1, we have argued that those investors who initiate the formation of a syndicate are more likely to have a need for additional screening re-sources (because they have a lower fit with the focal company). Conse-quently, we expect that these investors seek to acquire these lacking screen-ing resources through syndication, and those potential co-investors who can trade these resources (Hochberg et al., 2015) are thus more attractive partners. Consequently, we formulate:

Hypothesis 3: Those potential co-investors which have greater specialised expertise and a higher fit with the focal company are more likely to be invited to a syndi-cate.

5.3 Data, Variables, Sample and Methodology

5.3.1 Dataset

The empirical analysis in this study is based on a sample of VC invest-ments extracted from the VICO 4.0 dataset which has been created as a part of the RISIS research project promoted by the European Commission (see http://risis.eu for details). VICO 4.0 combines information on all exter-nal equity deals that occurred in the period 1998–2014 in companies locat-ed in European countries and Israel and reported by secondary informa-tion sources such as Zephyr, Crunchbase, and Thomson One. For further details please refer to Section 4.3.1.

Drawing on VICO 4.0 allows us to analyse realised as opposed to intend-ed investment strategies, as urged by De Clerq and Dimov (2004) and Jääskeläinen (2012) (i.e. we are using large-scale secondary data and do not conduct a survey in which we ask investors about their intended syndica-tion behaviour). Moreover, our rich time-series data allows us to employ robust econometric techniques to address potential endogeneity. Building on VICO 4.0, we follow a three-step approach to come up with our regres-sion sample. First, we calculate our specialisation metric (see next section for a detailed definition), which requires a 5-year trailing period (up to t-5). Consequently, we focus on funding rounds that occur between 2003 and 2014, and include only funding rounds from companies which raised their first round of funding during that time. Moreover, since VICO 4.0 is limi-ted to investment rounds in Europe and Israel and the calculation of our specialisation metric requires full transparency about investors' funding history, we focus our analysis on funding rounds from companies that are funded by European or Israeli investors. This leaves us with a base sample, which we use to build the regression samples for our different analyses. As we use different samples, variables and methods throughout the paper, we discuss the respective sample construction, variables and methods separately in the sub-sections below.

5.3.2 Sample Construction, Variables and Methods

Sample construction, variables and methods for analyses on syndicate formation

To test Hypotheses 1 and 2, we analyse the decision to form a syndicate from the perspective of the lead investor. The unit of analysis in our main sample is the funding round. Our regression sample includes 2,191 investments of lead investors. For each of the 2,191, we have one observation in our sample, and this observation stems either from a sole investor or, in cases where a syndicate was formed, from the lead investor of the syndicate. Following standard practices in syndication research, we define the lead investor as the investor who makes the largest investment in a given round (Hochberg et al., 2007). The reliable identification of lead investors thus places high demands on data, as it requires that the individual funding amounts of all investors in a syndicate are known precisely (and the individual amounts are not simply estimated using a pro rata heuristic, which is unfortunately often the case in conventional databases).

Our dependent variable *Syndicate* is a dummy equal to 1 if a funding round is syndicated, and 0 otherwise. Our main independent variable is the *Index of competitive advantage (ICA)*, a variable that jointly accounts for an investor's industry specialisation and the fit of this specialisation to the focal company. We build on the approach from Cressy et al. (2007), who use the *ICA* to determine a specialisation metric for their analysis of the effects of investor specialisation on portfolio companies' performance after private equity buyout transactions. The proxy is particularly well suited for our analyses, as it accounts for the fit between VC investors and the focal company and thus addresses the fact that the value of investors' specialised expertise depends on the context in which it is applied (see Lungeanu and Zajac, 2016 for a similar reasoning). Similar to Cressy et al. (2007), we define specialisation accordingly as an index of competitive advantage (ICA) – a construct that is based on the literature on international trade and technological specialisation (Archibugi and Pianta, 1994). Specifically, we define ICA for the VC sector as:

$$ICA_{i,t,y} = (F_{ity}/F_{.ty})/(F_{it}/F_{.t})$$

where:

F_{ity} is the number of companies in industry y that VC firm i invested in during the period t-5 to t-0;

$F_{.ty}$ is the total number of companies in industry y that all VC firms invested in during the period t-5 to t-0;

F_{it} is the total number of companies that VC firm i invested in during the period t-5 to t-0 and

$F_{.t}$ is the total number of companies that all VC firms invested in during the period t-5 to t-0.

The numerator of ICA represents a VC firm's share of all investments in an industry, and the denominator captures its share of all investments made in the market. For each investor in period t, we consider the investment track record from t-5 to t-0 to calculate the ICA for each industry. This means that the industry ICA of an investor is time-variant.[25] Moreover, given the importance of meaningful industry classifications that reflect the specific thematic expertise and knowledge through which investors can gain a competitive advantage, we manually aggregate NACE-industries into more thematic industries (for example, medical/health/life sciences) and use these for the ICA calculation.

Besides that, we use a number of controls. *Ln(Funding)* controls for the (natural logarithm) of the total funding round size, as the risk sharing motive is particularly acute when the investment is large (Hopp, 2010). *Past deals fund* captures the number of investments the lead investor conducted in the 5 years prior to the investment round at hand, and proxies for investors' size and experience. First, greater experience may reduce information asymmetries for investors and thus also reduce the need to syndicate to acquire additional screening resources. Moreover, smaller VC investors, all else being equal, have greater exposure to the risk associated with individual investments (Manigart et al., 2006) and thus the risk sharing motive translates into a higher propensity to syndicate. *Ln(Distance)* is the natural

---

25 If an investor has completed less than 10 investments overall, ICA is set to 0, since the investor's track record is insufficient to assess its specialisation and we do not want to conflate specialisation with inexperience.

logarithm of the geographic distance between the lead investor and the company at hand. It is an important control, as greater distance increases information problems and makes monitoring more difficult (e.g., Bernstein et al., 2016), which in turn makes syndication more likely. *Round number* is a proxy for the maturity of the company, as the propensity to syndicate varies across the lifetime of a company (Ferrary, 2010). *Age* captures company age, since the degree of informational asymmetries is greater for younger companies, which in turn affects the need for screening resources (Sapienza et al., 1996; Plummer et al., 2015). Moreover, we control for the type of investor (e.g., CVC investors vs. IVC investors), as different investor types may show differences in their syndication behaviour and specialisation. Finally, we additionally control for the company nation, company industry, investment years and investor nation to proxy for differences in the institutional environment, industry differences in company risk and changes over time.

In terms of identification strategy, we resort to standard probit regressions with robust standard errors, given that our dependent variable is dichotomous. For the analyses regarding Hypothesis 2, which include interaction terms, we provide additional analyses that were suggested by Ai and Norton (2003) and Norton et al. (2004) to determine the correct marginal effects and investigate the significance of the interaction term. That is required, as the sign and significance of regression coefficients does not allow for the same inferences as in linear regressions and might even be misleading (Hoetker, 2007).

We complement our main empirical approach with additional analyses that account for the potential endogeneity of VC investors' specialisation and syndication behaviour (Buchner et al., 2017). Specifically, we need to rule out the possibility of our results being affected by the potential endogeneity of the relationship between VC investors' degree of specialisation and their propensity to syndicate, as it is possible that VC investors' strategy (which we are unable to observe) affects both their degree of specialisation and their propensity to syndicate. Therefore, we resort to the GMM-SYS approach (Arellano and Bover, 1995; Blundell and Bond, 1998) to address the potential endogeneity. We use GMM-SYS with finite-sample correction (Windmeijer, 2005)[26] and implement it with a software package provided by Roodman (2006). This approach is econometrically highly ro-

---

26 Although the employed two-step estimator is asymptotically more efficient than the alternative one-step variant, the reported two-step standard errors are typically downward biased (Arellano and Bond, 1991; Blundell and Bond, 1998). There-

bust and practically established in the VC literature (Samila and Sorenson, 2011; Croce et al., 2013; Grilli and Murtinu, 2014). In the GMM-SYS analyses, we use the lags of the periods t-3 to t-5 as instruments for the potentially endogenous VC investor and company characteristics. The start in t-3 is justified by the results of the Arellano-Bond tests (please refer to Table 28, Columns 3 and 4, for the exact test statistics), showing that for the third lag, no autocorrelation is observed, which would otherwise invalidate these lags as instruments (Roodman, 2009). Moreover, we limit the number of lags to t-5 in order to avoid finite-sample bias, which could be caused by an excessively large number of instruments (Roodman, 2009; for an application in related research see Grilli and Murtinu, 2014). Finally, we routinely test the validity of our overidentifying restrictions (i.e. the exogeneity of our instruments) with the Hansen J-statistic.

As the GMM-SYS approach requires a panel dataset, we adapt our dataset accordingly. Specifically, we collapse our complete base sample (i.e. including all investment rounds) to construct investor-year observations that contain the yearly average values of the regression variables for an investor. For example, the observation for investor *i* in year *t* would include the average *ICA* of all investments that investor *i* has completed in year *t* along with the average value of all other regression variables such as *Syndication, ln(Past deals), ln(Distance)* etc. While using investor-year observations is less granular than an analysis at the deal level and the aggregation may hide certain variation, this approach is a prerequisite for the use of GMM-SYS and thus allows us to conduct an important robustness check of our main findings to rule out the possibility of endogeneity affecting these results. The final regression sample consists of 2,553 investor-year observations from 911 different investors.

Sample construction, variables and methods for analysis on syndicate partner choice

To assess the role of potential co-investors' specialised expertise for their attractiveness as syndicate partners (i.e. Hypothesis 3), we construct another dataset tailored to the specific analyses. Again, we evaluate the decision from the perspective of the lead investor. The idea is to evaluate how lead

---

fore, in all GMM regressions, we apply the finite-sample correction for the two-step covariance matrix that was suggested by Windmeijer (2005) for this case and which Roodman (2006) makes available in his software package.

investors choose their co-investor(s) and to assess if a co-investor's specialised expertise and fit with the focal company affect the probability that the particular co-investor is invited to a syndicate. Consequently, we construct a dataset in which we create dyads between the lead investors of syndicated investments and *all possible* co-investors (i.e. all other European investors in our dataset that were active at the time). The final sample consists of 175,908 observations.

Our dependent variable is *It's a match* – a dummy variable that identifies those lead investor–co-investor combinations that materialised in a given financing round (i.e. to identify those co-investors that the lead investor invited, and that joined the round) and distinguish them from the other possible lead investor–co-investor dyads.

Our main independent variable is *ICA_coinvestor*, which defines the fit of the specialised industry expertise of the potential co-investor with the focal venture. Moreover, we control for the size and experience of potential co-investors using *Past deals coinvestor*, which captures all deals the co-investor completed in the period t-5 to t-0. Similarly, we control for the commensurate industry experience using *Industry deals coinvestor*, which accounts for all deals the co-investor completed in the period t-5 to t-0 in the industry of the company at hand (Hopp, 2010). Moreover, we add *Prior interaction*, which is a dummy equal to 1, if the respective lead investor and co-investor have syndicated with one another in the past, as this is a strong predictor for future interactions (Lockett and Wright, 1999; Hopp and Lukas, 2014). In addition, we control for the geospatial distance between the lead investor and the potential co-investor (*ln(Lead–co distance)*) as spatial proximity facilitates the collaboration of investors in a syndicate network (Fritsch and Schilder, 2008). Moreover, we control for the type of co-investor (e.g., CVC vs. IVC), as the investor types may differ in their attractiveness as syndicate partners. Finally, we control for the nationality of the co-investor to account for institutional differences.

To implement our regressions, we again employ a standard probit model, and complement it with a rare events logistics model (Firth, 1993) to ensure the robustness of our findings, as the ratio of possible to actual investor dyads is about 700:1.

5.3.3 Sample Overview and Descriptive Statistics

Before turning to our analyses, we first provide a statistical summary and correlation matrix of our base sample in Table 27. The statistical summary demonstrates that our base sample is well balanced and suited for our purpose. For instance, the average of the syndication dummy is 0.48, which is in line with prior research, finding that around 40%–50% of the deals are syndicated in the European VC market (Wright and Lockett, 2003). Moreover, the median of *ICA* is very close to one, while the average of 2.09 is in line with the conventional wisdom that VC investors tend to specialise. Moreover, companies in our base sample are very young, with an average age of 4.67 years, and our sample includes their first investment rounds (with 1.58 being the median *Round number*) in our base sample. Finally, IVCs form the majority of investors, followed by GVCs. Besides that, the correlation between the regression variables is low, such that we find no evidence that the regression analyses would suffer from issues of multicollinearity (Wooldridge, 2009).

5.4 Empirical Analyses and Results

In this section we present our results. We start with the analyses on syndicate formation (Table 28 as well as Figures 1–3) and then turn to the analyses of the choice of syndicate partners (Table 29).

Table 28, Column 1 shows the probit regression for syndicate formation by the lead investor. The coefficient of interest is the one for *ICA*, as it captures an investor's industry specialisation and the fit with the focal company. The coefficient is negative and significant at the 5% level, which suggests that lead investors are less likely to syndicate an investment if their specialisation and fit with the focal company is higher, which is in line with Hypothesis 1. Column 3 presents the corresponding GMM-SYS analysis, which relies on an alternative sample construction procedure (see Section 5.3.2.1. for details). Again, the coefficient for *ICA* is negative and significant at the 5% level, which implies that the finding is robust to additional precautions to endogeneity. However, it is noteworthy that the interpretation of the coefficients in the GMM-SYS differs slightly from those in the probit regressions, since the unit of analysis varies. In the probit regressions, the unit of analysis is the lead investor's decision to syndicate a particular deal, whereas the GMM-SYS regressions, due to the aggregation of yearly data, capture investors' average propensity to pursue syndicated

Table 27: *Variable overview and correlation matrix*

Variable	Mean	SD	Me-dian	Min	Max	1	2	3	4	5	6	7	8	9	10	11	12	13
1 Syndicate dummy	0.48	0.50	0.00	0.00	1.00	1.00												
2 ICA	2.09	3.31	1.23	0.00	26.53	-0.05	1.00											
3 Age	5.14	4.67	4.00	0.00	26.00	-0.04	0.08	1.00										
4 ln(Past deals)	2.98	1.29	3.09	0.00	6.62	0.07	-0.03	-0.03	1.00									
5 Round number	1.58	1.09	1.00	1.00	11.00	0.16	0.12	0.07	0.14	1.00								
6 ln(Funding)	0.60	1.34	0.77	-3.30	3.43	0.28	0.04	0.11	-0.01	0.04	1.00							
7 ln(Distance)	4.02	2.18	4.61	-9.26	8.80	0.05	0.01	0.09	0.11	0.04	0.05	1.00						
8 IVC	0.67	0.47	1.00	0.00	1.00	-0.02	-0.01	0.03	-0.06	0.08	0.08	0.01	1.00					
9 CVC	0.04	0.19	0.00	0.00	1.00	-0.02	-0.01	-0.02	-0.07	-0.02	0.05	0.03	-0.29	1.00				
10 BVC	0.07	0.26	0.00	0.00	1.00	0.00	0.03	0.11	-0.08	-0.04	0.05	-0.02	-0.40	-0.06	1.00			
11 GVC	0.17	0.38	0.00	0.00	1.00	0.05	0.02	-0.05	0.21	-0.04	-0.09	0.03	-0.64	-0.09	-0.13	1.00		
12 OtherVC	0.03	0.18	0.00	0.00	1.00	-0.03	-0.01	-0.09	-0.06	-0.04	-0.06	-0.08	-0.27	-0.04	-0.05	-0.09	1.00	
13 UVC	0.02	0.12	0.00	0.00	1.00	0.00	-0.03	-0.05	-0.05	0.01	-0.11	-0.04	-0.18	-0.03	-0.04	-0.06	-0.02	1.00

Table 28: Probit and GMM-SYS regression analyses of syndicate formation

Variable	Main sample		GMM-SYS sample	
	(1)	(2)	(3)	(4)
	Probit	**Probit**	**GMM-SYS**	**GMM-SYS**
ICA	-0.0378**	-0.0626***	-0.0240**	-0.0415***
	(-2.319)	(-3.158)	(-2.298)	(-2.685)
Age	-0.0163*	-0.0261***	-0.0108***	-0.0197***
	(-1.851)	(-2.631)	(-3.204)	(-3.113)
ICA#Age		0.00407**		0.00389*
		(2.439)		(1.670)
ln(Past deals)	0.120***	0.123***	0.0365	0.0240
	(3.219)	(3.308)	(1.248)	(0.821)
Round number	0.243***	0.244***	0.0178	0.0348
	(6.823)	(6.819)	(0.658)	(1.457)
ln(Funding)	0.281***	0.285***	0.124***	0.131***
	(8.192)	(8.291)	(5.143)	(4.962)
ln(Distance)	0.0298	0.0287	0.0123	0.0106
	(1.429)	(1.369)	(0.673)	(0.615)
CVC	0.101	0.108	0.985*	0.606
	(0.401)	(0.428)	(1.911)	(1.373)
BVC	0.0627	0.0606	-0.396	-0.227
	(0.390)	(0.373)	(-1.518)	(-1.147)
GVC	0.197	0.194	-0.269	-0.207
	(1.558)	(1.528)	(-1.518)	(-1.307)
OtherVC	0.951***	0.965***	-0.248	-0.220
	(4.021)	(4.079)	(-0.706)	(-0.689)
UVC	0.413	0.402	0.551	0.422
	(1.255)	(1.222)	(1.336)	(1.138)
Constant	-1.769***	-1.727***	0.568***	0.609***
	(-8.282)	(-8.000)	(4.692)	(5.836)
Company nation FE	YES	YES	YES	YES
Company industry FE	YES	YES	YES	YES
Year FE	YES	YES	YES	YES
Investor nation FE	YES	YES	YES	YES
AR1 p-value	-	-	0	0

Variable	Main sample		GMM-SYS sample	
	(1)	(2)	(3)	(4)
	Probit	Probit	GMM-SYS	GMM-SYS
AR2 p-value	-	-	0.722	0.906
AR3 p-value	-	-	0.671	0.695
Hansen J-statistic p-value	-	-	0.918	0.850
N	2,191	2,191	2,553	2,553

Table 28 shows probit and GMM-SYS regressions of investors' propensity to form a syndicate. Regressions 1 and 2 are standard probit regressions with robust standard errors, Regressions 3 and 4 are GMM-SYS regressions (two-step system generalised method of moments estimator) with finite-sample correction. *ICA* captures investors' industry specialisation and fit with the focal venture. *ICA#Age* is an interaction term of *ICA* and the age of the focal venture. Further details and the definition of the remaining variables are presented in Section 5.3.2. Please note that the probit and GMM-SYS regressions use different samples and the variables in the GMM-SYS regressions represent investor-year averages – the details of this procedure are described in Section 5.3.2. Robust z and t-statistics, respectively, are reported in parentheses. *, ** and *** denote statistical significance at the 10%, 5% and 1% level, respectively.

deals in a given year. However, the results support the same conclusion: the greater the fit between a venture capitalist and a prospective investment, the less likely the investor is to syndicate the deal.

The analyses of the moderating effect of venture age on the relationship between *ICA* and *Syndication* are shown in Columns 2 and 4 of Table 28. Column 2 shows the probit regression. While the coefficient for *ICA* remains negative and even becomes significant at the 1% level, the coefficient for the interaction term *ICA#Age* is positive and significant at the 5% level. However, further analyses are required to interpret this finding reliably. Caution is needed when interpreting the regression results of the interaction effects in non-linear probit regressions, because the sign and significance of regression coefficients does not allow for the same inferences as in linear regressions and might even be misleading (Hoetker, 2007). For instance, Ai and Norton (2003) show that the magnitude and significance of an interaction effect can vary by observation – i.e. that it can be negative and significant for some observations and positive and significant for others. Therefore, a graphical representation may be best suited to interpret the results (Hoetker, 2007). We hence build on the graphical representation of Ai and Norton (2003) and investigate the interaction effects graphically in Figures 1 and 2 by using a software package provided by Norton et al. (2004). Figure 1 shows the interaction effect as a function of the predicted probability for syndication. It plots the interaction effect (i.e. the magnitude of the coefficient) for each observation against the probability that the dependent dichotomous variable is equal to 1.

Figure 1: Scatterplot of the interaction effect ICA#Age in the probit regression

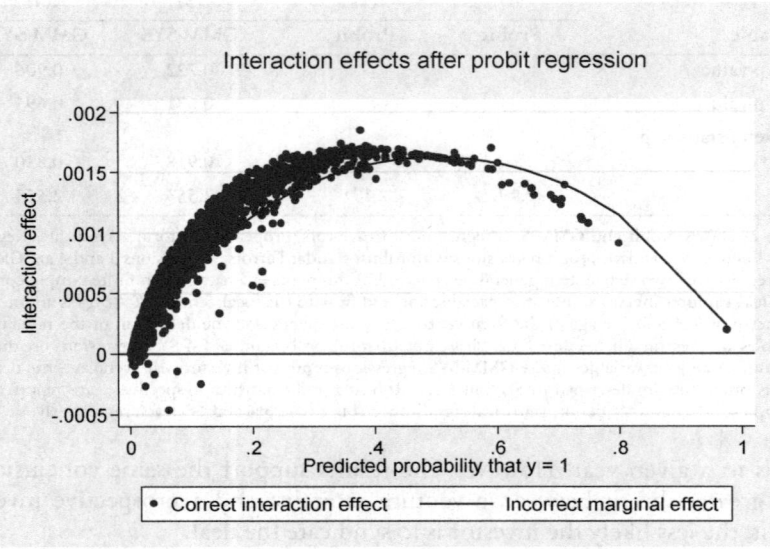

Figure 2: Scatterplot of the z-statistics for the interaction effect ICA#Age in the probit regression

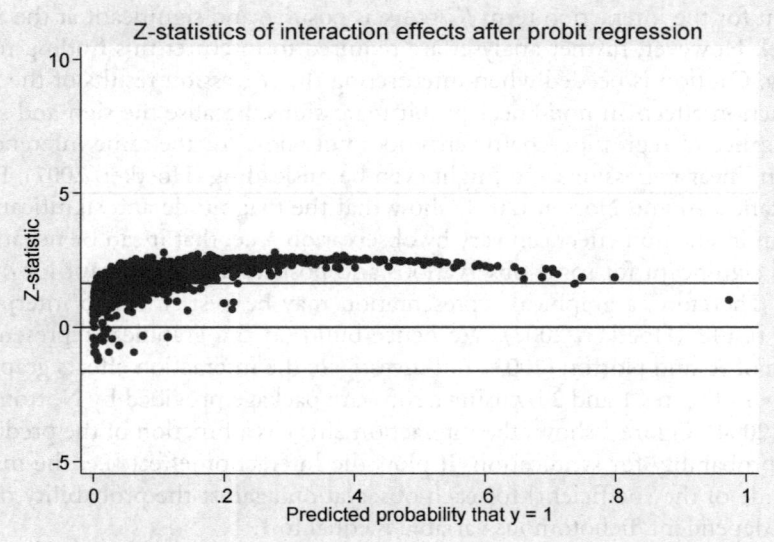

Figure 3: Graphical illustration of the predicted probability to syndicate as a function of ICA and company age

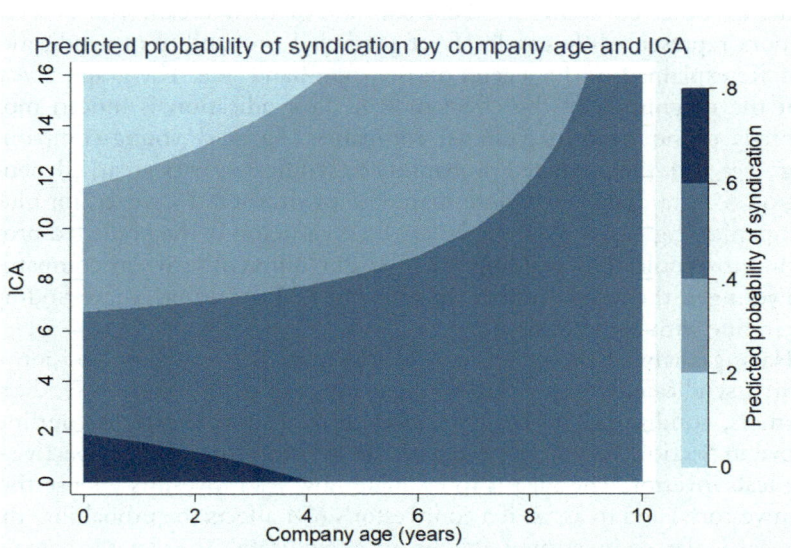

Figure 2 plots the z-statistics of each observation accordingly, and the red lines in the graph mark the thresholds for significance at the 10% level. We can infer from the graphs that the interaction effect is indeed positive and significant for many observations, especially for those with a medium to high probability of being syndicated (i.e. a predicted probability between 0.2 and 0.8) while 0 observations have a negative and significant interaction effect. In additional analyses using the software package from Norton et al. (2004), we are able to identify these observations individually – 1,319 (888) out of 2,191 observations are positive and significant at the 10% (5%) level while 872 are insignificant. Thus, it is reasonable to conclude that there is indeed a positive interaction effect for the majority of cases. Besides that, the positive significance of the interaction term is also confirmed in the alternative GMM-SYS regression (Table 28, Column 4), where the interaction term *ICA#Age* is positive and significant, too – although the significance level is lower, at 10%.

However, the interpretation of the interaction term of the two continuous variables *ICA* and *Age* is not trivial, given that the interaction term is positive, while the coefficients for both individual variables are negative. Therefore, we provide a graphical illustration that simplifies the understanding of the interaction terms. Figure 3 is a graphical illustration of the predicted probability to syndicate as a function of *ICA* and company *Age* while all other covariates are held constant at their mean. The different colours represent different levels of predicted probability of syndication and are explained in the legend on the right-hand side. The graph reveals that the magnitude of the effect of *ICA* on syndication is indeed more strongly pronounced for younger companies. For very young companies (e.g., *Age* = 1), the predicted probability to syndicate varies greatly depending on *ICA*, ranging from more than 60% to almost 0. However, for older companies (e.g., *Age* = 8), there is very little variation in the predicted probability to syndicate depending on *ICA*. Put differently: when companies are younger, the magnitude of the effect of *ICA* is greater. These findings are in line with Hypothesis 2.

Having analysed the effect of lead investors' *ICA* on their decision to form a syndicate, we now turn to the analysis of their choice of syndicate partners, conditional on their decision to form a syndicate. As outlined above in Section 5.3.2.2., we evaluate the decision from the perspective of the lead investor. The idea is to evaluate how lead investors choose their co-investor(s) and to assess if a co-investor's *ICA* affects the probability that the particular co-investor is invited to a syndicate. The dataset contains 175,908 possible lead investor–co-investor dyads and the binary dependent variable *It's a match* identifies those dyads that actually occurred. The results of the regressions are presented in Table 29. Column 1 shows the results of the probit regression. The variable of interest is *ICA_coinvestor* as it captures a potential co-investor's industry specialisation and its fit with the focal company. The coefficient for *ICA_coinvestor* is positive and significant at the 1% level. Thus, this result provides evidence suggesting that those potential co-investors that have a high degree of specialisation and fit with the focal venture are more likely to be chosen as co-investors. It is noteworthy, that the regression also includes several controls for important co-investor characteristics, such as prior interactions between the lead and potential co-investor (Lockett and Wright, 1999; Hopp and Lukas, 2014) as well as co-investors' industry experience (Hopp, 2010). Moreover, the findings are robust to the use of a rare events logistics model (Firth, 1993) shown in Column 2, which accounts for the fact that very few of the possible lead–co-investor dyads actually occurred.

Table 29: Probit and firthlogit regressions of co-investor choice

	(1)	(2)
Variable	**Probit**	**Firthlogit**
ICA_coinvestor	0.0353***	0.0728***
	(5.524)	(7.489)
Prior interaction	0.670***	1.894***
	(8.750)	(9.626)
ln(Past deals coinvestor)	0.0643***	0.252***
	(2.703)	(3.265)
ln(Industry deals coinvestor)	0.195***	0.500***
	(6.931)	(6.058)
ln(Lead-co distance)	-0.0964***	-0.249***
	(-6.720)	(-6.620)
CVC_coinvestor	-0.0751	-0.328
	(-0.572)	(-0.854)
BVC_coinvestor	0.0306	0.0461
	(0.319)	(0.172)
GVC_coinvestor	0.252***	0.826***
	(3.885)	(4.373)
OtherVC_coinvestor	0.214*	0.759**
	(1.795)	(2.077)
UVC_coinvestor	0.263*	0.985**
	(1.826)	(2.134)
Coinvestor nation FE	YES	YES
Constant	-3.028***	-6.654***
	(-12.90)	(-9.660)
N	175,908	175,908

Table 29 shows probit and rare events logit (Firth, 1993) regressions of the materialisation of possible lead investor-co-investor dyads. *ICA_coinvestor* captures co-investors' industry specialisation and fit with the focal venture. Further details and the definition of the remaining variables are presented in Section 5.3.2. Robust z-statistics are reported in parentheses. *, ** and *** denote statistical significance at the 10%, 5% and 1% level, respectively.

5.5 Discussion

The syndication of investments is a characteristic feature of the VC industry (Wright and Lockett, 2003; Ferrary, 2010). However, lead investors' decisions and motivations to initiate the formation of a syndicate are not sufficiently understood to date and the antecedents of this decision are underexplored (Jääskeläinen, 2012). In this paper, we investigate empirically what drives investors' decisions to share a *particular* investment opportunity with co-investors and to undertake others individually by analysing specialised investor–company-fit as an antecedent of the decision to syndicate at the deal level. Moreover, our empirical analysis links lead investors' decision to form a syndicate with their subsequent choice of syndicate partners and thus creates a novel, integrated perspective on the formation of syndicates (De Clerq and Dimov, 2004; Manigart et al., 2006) and the composition of syndicates (Hopp and Lukas, 2014; Hochberg et al., 2015; Gompers et al., 2016 b). Our research makes three important findings.

First, we find that greater specialisation and investor–firm-fit reduces lead investors' propensity to syndicate a deal, suggesting that specialised investor–company-fit reduces information asymmetries and therefore allows investors to make better informed investment decisions. This explanation is consistent with arguments suggesting that greater specialisation and investor–company-fit reduce critical information asymmetries for investors (Casamatta and Haritchabalet, 2007; Gompers et al., 2009). It also supports arguments according to which investors syndicate if their own evaluation of the investment opportunity is insufficient to come up with a clear decision whether or not to pursue the investment and they thus prefer to get a second opinion by another venture capitalist (Lerner, 1994; Brander et al., 2002). However, it is important to stress that our findings provide novel and robust empirical evidence that overcomes the shortcomings of the limited prior empirical research on the link between specialisation and syndication. For instance, our findings complement those of Manigart et al. (2006), Hopp (2010) and De Clerq and Dimov (2004) who relied on suboptimal specialisation measures and neglected the importance of investor–company-fit (Lungeanu and Zajac, 2016), and either used aggregate (De Clerq and Dimov, 2004) or primary data (Manigart et al., 2006), which may thus hamper their empirics – for instance, Mangiart et al. (2006) acknowledge that research using a more fine-grained measure of VC specialisation is in order. Consequently, it is noteworthy to compare our results to those from prior research. Interestingly, our findings are qualitatively very similar to those of Manigart et al. (2006) and De Clerq and Dimov (2004), as these researchers also find a negative relationship between investors' degree of specialisation and their propensity to syndicate, although our findings are stronger and also more robust. For instance, the findings of De Clerq and Dimov (2004) are only significant at the 10% level in one of their regression models and insignificant in the other one; and Manigart et al. (2006) only report significant findings for a subsample of early-stage investors. Thus, our more significant findings are likely explained by our methodological improvements. Moreover, our findings are also robust to an alternative estimation strategy that addresses potential endogeneity in the relationship between VC investors' degree of specialisation and their propensity to syndicate.

Our second important finding is that the effect of specialisation and investor–company-fit on the decision to syndicate is more pronounced for investments in younger companies. This is interesting and intuitively intriguing, as it suggests that the positive effect of greater investor–company-fit on screening capabilities is of greater value in situations where information asymmetries are particularly large. Moreover, this finding could explain why Manigart et al. (2006) only find a relation between investor specialisation and the propensity to syndicate for screening purposes in a particular subsample containing early-stage investors.

Third, the relevance of investor–company-fit for investment selection is highlighted by the fact that investor–company-fit is also a significant determinant of the choice of co-investors. Specifically, we find that, when syndicating, lead investors are more likely to select those potential co-investors as syndicate partners that have a higher fit with the venture at hand. This result suggests that investor–company-fit is a critical factor for the attractiveness of potential co-investors, and the finding is present despite several controls for important co-investor characteristics, such as prior interactions between the lead and potential co-investor (Lockett and Wright, 1999; Hopp and Lukas, 2014) as well as co-investors' industry experience (Hopp, 2010). This finding is highly interesting for several reasons. It provides, to the best of our knowledge, the first evidence for the integrated relationship between the decision to syndicate and the choice of co-investors, and thus reveals the opportunistic nature of lead investors' decision to syndicate. Moreover, it adds to a better understanding of the formation and dynamics of syndicates and syndicate networks (Milanov and Shepherd, 2013; Hopp and Lukas, 2014; Hochberg et al., 2015; Gompers et al., 2016 b) and provides supporting evidence for the notion that investors seek to acquire complementary resources through syndication (Hochberg et al., 2015).

This research makes several contributions to the literature. First, our findings contribute to the literature on VC syndication (e.g., Manigart et al., 2006; Hochberg et al., 2015), as we provide a fine-grained, empirically-backed understanding of investors' decisions and motivations to syndicate *particular deals*, which has been missing in prior research (Jääaskelainen, 2012). In addition, our research provides a novel perspective on the integrated relationship between the decision to syndicate and the choice of co-investors, and reveals the opportunistic nature of lead investors' decision to syndicate. Moreover, we add to the literature that attempts to understand VC investors' screening and decision-making processes (Kirsch et al., 2009; Petty and Gruber, 2011), as our findings suggest that specialised investor–company-fit is a valuable resource for investment decisions, as it shapes lead investors' decisions to form a syndicate as well as the attractiveness of potential partners. Finally, we add to the literature on specialisation (vs. diversification) as VC investment strategy (e.g., Gompers et al., 2009; Matusik and Fitza, 2012; Buchner et al., 2017) by linking it with the literature on syndication and providing a more holistic understanding of the implications of VC strategy for VC investors' deal structuring while tackling the shortcomings of prior research.

As is inevitable, this research entails certain limitations that offer avenues for future research. First, our sample size is limited by the fact that existing data sources make it difficult to reliably identify the lead investor of a syndicate. Conventionally, researchers identify the lead investor as the one making the largest investment in a given round (e.g., Hochberg et al., 2007), but in practice the individual investment amounts of VC investors are estimated by the database providers and these often apply pro rata estimates, such that the lead investor cannot be determined in these cases. Therefore, using private or hand-collected data could be a worthwhile extension of this research. Moreover, in the hypothesis development and results interpretation, this paper makes an implicit simplification, as it considers specialisation and investor–company-fit to be linked exclusively to investors' ex-ante risk reduction motive (Manigart et al., 2006) and thus neglects the possibility that the investor–company-fit could potentially affect other motives, especially the value-adding motive, too. While it is impossible to disentangle the underlying motives using secondary data – which provides other distinct advantages compared to survey data (De Clerq and Dimov, 2004; Jääskeläinen, 2012) – a research design combining both primary and secondary data could yield even more detailed insights and combine the advantages of the different data types. Finally, our analyses on partner choice are somewhat simplistic due to the fact that we are only able to observe those syndicates that have materialised. Therefore, certain complexities of this multi-stage and multi-party process, such as negotiations with potential co-investors that did not materialise, a potential effect of the lead investors' *ICA* on the *lead* investors' attractiveness for co-investors or the role of entrepreneurs cannot be reflected. However, future research might be able to address these simplifications using richer data and a more complex model accounting for these potential interdependencies.

5.6 Conclusion

The syndication of investments is one of the characteristic features of the VC industry (Wright and Lockett, 2003; Ferrary, 2010). However, lead investors' deal-specific reasons to initiate the formation of a syndicate are underexplored. In this paper, we analyse specialised investor–company-fit as an antecedent of investors' decisions to syndicate deals and additionally assess how investor–company-fit shapes the choice of co-investors and thus the composition of syndicates. We find that lead investors are less likely to syndicate a deal if their fit with the focal venture is higher, and this effect is more pronounced for younger ventures. However, when syndicating, lead investors are more likely to select as syndicate partners those potential co-investors that have a higher fit with the venture at hand. Our findings highlight that industry specialisation and investor–company-fit are important resources that reduce information asymmetries and therefore allow investors to make better informed investment decisions. Moreover, our findings reveal the opportunistic nature of lead investors' decisions to syndicate and support the notion that investors seek to acquire complementary resources when syndicating. This research contributes to the literature on VC syndication (e.g., Manigart et al., 2006; Hochberg et al., 2015) by substantiating investors' reasons to syndicate at the deal level and revealing the interrelation between investors' decisions to syndicate and their choice of co-investors. Additionally, it adds to the literature on VC investors' screening and decision-making processes (Kirsch et al., 2009; Petty and Gruber, 2011) by identifying specialised investor–company-fit as a valuable resource for investment decisions. Finally, we advance the literature on specialisation as a VC investment strategy (e.g., Gompers et al., 2009; Matusik and Fitza, 2012; Buchner et al., 2017) by linking it with the literature on syndication and thus providing a more holistic understanding of the implications of VC investors' strategy, investment decision process, and deal structuring.

6 Overall Conclusion and Contribution

As outlined, the research questions addressed in this dissertation are relevant for both academic researchers and practitioners. Hence, this chapter provides an overview and summary of the contributions of the research presented hitherto.

6.1 Theoretical Contribution

Taken together and regarded from a thematic perspective, this dissertation contributes to various aspects of the entrepreneurial equity financing literature and makes additional, selected contributions to adjacent research areas, such as organisational learning and openness. In a broader context, this dissertation adds to the resource-based view as well as agency cost theory.

First of all, this dissertation advances the literature on screening and value-added in entrepreneurial equity financing, in both breadth and depth. In terms of breadth, this research extends the literature stream on the value-adding effects of early-stage investors, which hitherto covered various types of venture capitalists (Chemmanur et al., 2011; Croce et al., 2013; Chemmanur et al., 2014; Grilli and Murtinu, 2014) and business angels (Kerr et al., 2013; Dutta and Folta, 2016), to equity crowdfunding, which is an increasingly important innovative funding mechanism for new ventures (Bruton et al., 2015; Vulkan et al., 2016; Signori and Vismara, 2018). Substantively, however, the results reveal that equity-crowdfunded companies' subsequent performance is causally negatively affected compared to peers using traditional entrepreneurial equity funding, since equity crowdfunding investors add less value than venture capitalists and angel investors. The findings are consistent with the notion that a combination of suboptimal monitoring, a more complex investor–company relationship – that currently fails to make use of crowd investors' potentially valuable managerial and social capital resources – as well as inferior investor reputation cause equity crowdfunders' inferior value-added. Therefore, the results of this essay are naturally also of importance for the nascent literature stream on crowdfunding, as they provide evidence that helps understand how crowdfunding impacts companies' pathways (Stanko and Henard,

2017; Dushnitsky and Zunino, 2018; Signori and Vismara, 2018). Furthermore, as an additional contribution, this research adds to the literature on openness (Hautz et al., 2017; Stanko and Henard, 2017) by proposing to complement 'open' funding practices (such as equity crowdfunding) with commensurate open strategy and innovation practices to make use of crowd investors' competencies and networks. Finally, the findings highlight that regulation is an important enabler for novel funding mechanisms such as equity crowdfunding and that it plays a triggering role for the adoption of these funding alternatives by high-profile entrepreneurs (Davidsson et al., 2018).

The second essay deepens the scientific knowledge on venture capitalists' screening and value-adding by providing evidence for heterogeneity among investors in their ability to select promising ventures and add value to them. To be precise, the essay advances the literature by providing evidence for a causal link between specific investor characteristics (investors' industry specialisation and the investor–company-fit) and value-added. Prior research on venture capitalists' value-added has examined differences between investors in terms of their type (e.g., comparing IVC investors to GVC or CVC investors; see e.g., Grilli and Murtinu, 2014 and Chemmanur et al., 2014) but evidence on other characteristics is scarce and much needed (Tykvová, 2018). Specifically, the analyses show that high levels of industry specialisation are detrimental to investors' value-added, suggesting that early-stage venture capitalists benefit from diverse experience rather than deep industry knowledge in their portfolio work, for instance because a diverse knowledge base may equip investors with superior problem-solving skills (Ahuja and Katila, 2001), foster analogical thinking (Gavetti et al., 2005) and also allows investors to advise companies on multiple trajectories (Matusik and Fitza, 2012). This finding is also of importance for related research from organisational learning (e.g., Matusik and Fitza, 2012), as it provides evidence on how investors can build their value-adding capabilities.

Moreover, the second essay indicates that there is heterogeneity among VC investors in their ability to select ventures with greater inherent growth potential, whilst accounting for endogeneity. While this finding is intuitively appealing, it provides new evidence, given that prior research on VC decision-making was more concerned with the question of how decisions are made (Kirsch et al., 2009; Petty and Gruber, 2011; Bernstein et al., 2017) and less with the quality of the decision outcome. Similarly, prior research on VC screening and value-added (e.g., Croce et al., 2013) typically measures screening effects between funded and non-funded companies and not within the group of companies funded by different VC investors.

The notion that greater specialisation and investor–company-fit positively affect venture capitalists' investment selection ability is also supported by the findings of the third essay. This research finds that investors are less likely to syndicate a deal if their fit with the focal venture is higher. However, conditional on the decision to syndicate, the lead investors are more likely to syndicate with those potential co-investors that have a higher fit with the focal venture. This empirical finding is thus consistent with theoretical arguments suggesting that specialised expertise is an important resource that reduces information asymmetries (Manigart et al., 2006) and therefore allows investors to make better informed investment decisions. Moreover, it suggests that lead investors seek to acquire complementary resources (Hochberg et al., 2015) when forming a syndicate. Thus, the essay informs the literature on VC syndication (e.g., Wright and Lockett, 2003; Jääskeläinen et al., 2006; Manigart et al., 2006; Hochberg et al., 2015), as it provides new large-scale empirical evidence for the antecedents of lead investors' decisions to syndicate particular deals and exposes the opportunistic reasons underlying the decision to syndicate, as well as the choice of syndicate partners.

Taken together, the findings on specialisation highlight the influence of venture capitalists' industry specialisation on outcomes across different stages of the investment process – ranging from deal selection and deal structuring to the post-investment value-added, which thus contributes to the literature on specialisation as a VC investment strategy (e.g., De Clercq and Dimov, 2006; Cressy et al., 2014; Humphery-Jenner, 2012; Buchner et al., 2017).

In the broader context of management research, the findings of this dissertation add to the resource-based view (Barney, 1991) as they identify specific resources that are valuable in the context of entrepreneurial finance. For instance, this research suggests that diverse rather than specialised expertise is a resource that improves venture capitalists' value-added, whereas industry specialisation combined with investor–company-fit is a valuable resource for investment selection purposes. Moreover, the findings from the equity crowdfunding essay underscore that the formal and informal channels through which entrepreneurs access their investors' networks and managerial capabilities are an important enabler for investors' resource provision. Besides that, the essay on equity crowdfunding also puts agency cost theory (Jensen and Meckling, 1976) into the context of new digital funding models, and thus validates the theory's ongoing relevance in the digital age.

6.2 Practical Contribution

This dissertation provides several implications for entrepreneurial finance practice, as its findings are of interest to entrepreneurs, operators of equity crowdfunding platforms and equity crowdfunders, regulators and policymakers, as well as venture capitalists.

First, the findings of this research inform entrepreneurs that seek to acquire equity capital and that can choose among multiple sources of funding. In order to draw most value from the investor–investee relationship and benefit from investors' value-adding contributions, start-ups should raise VC or angel financing rather than equity crowdfunding to avoid negative subsequent performance impacts compared to competitors that rely on VC or angel funding. Moreover, entrepreneurs can maximise their benefits from venture capitalists' value-added by raising capital from venture capitalists with a diverse, rather than specialised, industry experience and by avoiding the detrimental performance effects of a high investor–company-fit. For those entrepreneurs that rely on equity crowdfunding, it is indispensable to find ways to make use of their investors' networks and competencies – for instance by adopting open strategy practices to engage crowdfunders.

The results of this research should be a call for action for providers of equity crowdfunding platforms. To avoid an adverse selection of low-quality companies and to ensure the competitiveness of the companies that are funded on their platform, providers need to respond quickly and tackle the deficiencies that currently hamper equity-crowdfunded companies' post-funding performance. Platform providers should respond, for instance, by putting stronger monitoring measures in place. For example, they could send a representative of the crowd to the boards of funded companies, or by staging the payout of funds on the basis of milestones. Another example of the measures they could take would be to ensure that companies receive adequate post-funding support and advice – either through establishing an open strategy toolkit that draws on the competencies of crowd investors, or by building own competencies and sharing best practices among portfolio companies. Alternatively, instead of becoming more actively involved and emulating the value-adding of traditional investors, platform providers could partner with selected VC firms and syndicate deals with them (see

Agrawal et al., 2016 for a similar argument). In any case, providers of equity crowdfunding platforms have the strongest incentive to address both the observed adverse selection of low-quality companies and the inferior value-added of crowdfunders, as they might otherwise be running 'markets for lemons' and go out of business in the long run. However, before these changes become effective, equity crowdfunders (i.e. users investing on equity crowdfunding platforms) should be particularly careful when selecting companies to invest in, and bear in mind that these companies are likely to face a competitive disadvantage compared to seed and angel-funded peers in the post-funding period.

The empirical findings of this dissertation provide several implications for regulators and policymakers. First, in its current state, equity crowdfunding is no panacea for the scarcity of entrepreneurial risk capital and therefore, regulators and policymakers should respond with a dual strategy. On the one hand, it is required to tackle the current shortcomings in order to unlock further potential from equity crowdfunding. To do so, regulators could moderate part of the adverse selection problem by making equity crowdfunding more attractive for start-ups, for instance by allowing higher funding volumes. However, this task is not straightforward, as regulators need to account for investor protection, too. Nonetheless, regulators may be able to induce changes by platform providers and urge them to address the current deficits with respect to post-funding monitoring and value-added. However, on the other hand, more interventions are needed to provide additional funding options for entrepreneurs, and given the weaknesses and the existing risk of market failure for equity crowdfunding, policymakers should continue to leverage alternative options, such as GVCs and grants too. Besides that, when running a GVC, policymakers should encourage their GVC managers to follow a diverse investment strategy in order to maximise value-added for portfolio companies.

The main takeaway that this research offers to venture capitalists is that they need to identify and manage an optimal level of specialisation, as the results of this research suggest that venture capitalists face a trade-off: between acquiring strong industry specialisation, which helps them select high-potential companies, and diverse experience, which is beneficial for their value-added. Thus, fund managers need to strike a balance between selection and treatment effects in order to maximise fund returns given these boundary conditions. Besides that, VC firms can act on the findings by forming syndicates in which specialised VC firms focus on the selection and non-specialised firms focus on the operating value-added, as this would allow VC investors to potentially get the 'best of both worlds' by employing their skills in the best possible way. In fact, the results of the essay on syndication suggest that certain VC investors indeed already act accordingly and opportunistically form syndicate relationships to acquire investment selection capabilities.

7. References

Admati, Anat R.; Pfleiderer, Paul (1994): Robust financial contracting and the role of venture capitalists. In *The Journal of Finance* 49 (2), pp. 371–402.

Agrawal, Ajay; Catalini, Christian; Goldfarb, Avi (2014): Some simple economics of crowdfunding. In *Innovation Policy and the Economy* 14 (1), pp. 63–97.

Agrawal, Ajay; Catalini, Christian; Goldfarb, Avi (2015): Crowdfunding: Geography, social networks, and the timing of investment decisions. In *Journal of Economics & Management Strategy* 24 (2), pp. 253–274.

Agrawal, Ajay; Catalini, Christian; Goldfarb, Avi (2016): Are syndicates the killer app of equity crowdfunding? In *California Management Review* 58 (2), pp. 111–124.

Ahlers, Gerrit K.C.; Cumming, Douglas; Günther, Christina; Schweizer, Denis (2015): Signaling in equity crowdfunding. In *Entrepreneurship Theory and Practice* 39 (4), pp. 955–980.

Ahuja, Gautam; Katila, Riitta (2001): Technological acquisitions and the innovation performance of acquiring firms: A longitudinal study. In *Strategic Management Journal* 22 (3), pp. 197–220.

Ai, Chunrong; Norton, Edward C. (2003): Interaction terms in logit and probit models. In *Economics Letters* 80 (1), pp. 123–129.

Akerlof, George A. (1970): The market for 'lemons': Quality uncertainty and the market mechanism. In *The Quarterly Journal of Economics* 84 (3), p. 488-500.

Alexy, Oliver T.; Block, Joern H.; Sandner, Philipp; Ter Wal, Anne L. J. (2012): Social capital of venture capitalists and start-up funding. In *Small Business Economics* 39 (4), pp. 835–851.

Allison, Thomas H.; Davis, Blakley C.; Short, Jeremy C.; Webb, Justin W. (2015): Crowdfunding in a prosocial microlending environment: Examining the role of intrinsic versus extrinsic cues. In *Entrepreneurship Theory and Practice* 39 (1), pp. 53–73.

Amit, Raphael; Brander, James; Zott, Christoph (1998): Why do venture capital firms exist? Theory and Canadian evidence. In *Journal of Business Venturing* 13 (6), pp. 441–466.

Andrews, Donald W. K.; Moreira, Marcelo J.; Stock, James H. (2006): Optimal two-sided invariant similar tests for instrumental variables regression. In *Econometrica* 74 (3), pp. 715–752.

Archibugi, D.; Pianta, M. (1994): Aggregate convergence and sectoral specialisation in innovations. In *Journal of Evolutionary Economics* 4, pp. 17–33.

Arellano, Manuel; Bover, Olympia (1995): Another look at the instrumental variable estimation of error-components models. In *Journal of Econometrics* 68 (1), pp. 29–51.

Bapna, S.; Benner, M. J. (2014): Entrepreneurship, legitimacy and online social communities. An empirical analysis. In *Academy of Management Proceedings* 2014 (1).

Barney, Jay (1991): Firm resources and sustained competitive advantage. In *Journal of Management* 17 (1), pp. 99–120.

Bascle, Guilhem (2008): Controlling for endogeneity with instrumental variables in strategic management research. In *Strategic Organization* 6 (3), pp. 285–327.

Baum, Christopher F.; Schaffer, Mark E.; Stillman, Steven (2003): Instrumental variables and GMM: Estimation and testing. In *Stata Journal* 3 (1), pp. 1–31.

Baum, Joel A. C.; Silverman, Brian S. (2004): Picking winners or building them? Alliance, intellectual, and human capital as selection criteria in venture financing and performance of biotechnology startups. In *Journal of Business Venturing* 19 (3), pp. 411–436.

Belleflamme, Paul; Lambert, Thomas; Schwienbacher, Armin (2014): Crowdfunding: Tapping the right crowd. In *Journal of Business Venturing* 29 (5), pp. 585–609.

Berger, Allen N.; Udell, Gregory F. (1998): The economics of small business finance: The roles of private equity and debt markets in the financial growth cycle. In *Journal of Banking and Finance* 22 (6–8), pp. 613–673.

Bernstein, Shai; Giroud, Xavier; Townsend, Richard R. (2016): The impact of venture capital monitoring. In *The Journal of Finance* 71 (4), pp. 1591–1622.

Bernstein, Shai; Korteweg, Arthur; Laws, Kevin (2017): Attracting early-stage investors: Evidence from a randomized field experiment. In *The Journal of Finance* 72 (2), pp. 509–538.

Bertoni, Fabio; Colombo, Massimo G.; Grilli, Luca (2011): Venture capital financing and the growth of high-tech start-ups: Disentangling treatment from selection effects. In *Research Policy* 40 (7), pp. 1028–1043.

Binks, Martin R.; Ennew, Christine T. (1996): Growing firms and the credit constraint. In *Small Business Economics* 8 (1), pp. 17–25.

Black, Bernard S.; Gilson, Ronald J. (1998): Venture capital and the structure of capital markets. In *Journal of Financial Economics* 47 (3), pp. 243–277.

Block, Jörn; Colombo, Massimo G.; Cumming, Douglas J.; Vismara, Silvio (2018a): New players in entrepreneurial finance and why they are there. In *Small Business Economics* 50 (2), pp. 239–250.

Block, Jörn; Fisch, Christian O.; van Praag, Mirjam (2017): The Schumpeterian entrepreneur: A review of the empirical evidence on the antecedents, behaviour and consequences of innovative entrepreneurship. In *Industry and Innovation* 24 (1), pp. 61–95.

Block, Jörn; Hornuf, Lars; Moritz, Alexandra (2018b): Which updates during an equity crowdfunding campaign increase crowd participation? In *Small Business Economics* 50 (1), pp. 3–27.

Block, Jörn; Sandner, Philipp (2009): What is the effect of the financial crisis on venture capital financing? Empirical evidence from US Internet start-ups. In *Venture Capital* 11 (4), pp. 295–309.

Blundell, Richard; Bond, Stephen (1998): Initial conditions and moment restrictions in dynamic panel data models. In *Journal of Econometrics* 87 (1), pp. 115–143.

Brander, James A.; Amit, Raphael; Antweiler, Werner (2002): Venture-capital syndication: Improved venture selection vs. the value-added hypothesis. In *Journal of Economics & Management Strategy* 11 (3), pp. 423–452.

Breusch, T. S.; Pagan, A. R. (1979): A simple test for heteroscedasticity and random coefficient variation. In *Econometrica* 47 (5), p. 1287–1294.

Bruton, Garry; Khavul, Susanna; Siegel, Donald; Wright, Mike (2015): New financial alternatives in seeding entrepreneurship: Microfinance, crowdfunding, and peer-to-peer innovations. In *Entrepreneurship Theory and Practice* 39 (1), pp. 9–26.

Buchner, Axel; Mohamed, Abdulkadir; Schwienbacher, Armin (2017): Diversification, risk, and returns in venture capital. In *Journal of Business Venturing* 32 (5), pp. 519–535.

Burtch, Gordon; Ghose, Anindya; Wattal, Sunil (2015): The hidden cost of accommodating crowdfunder privacy preferences: A randomized field experiment. In *Management Science* 61 (5), pp. 949–962.

Bygrave, William D. (1987): Syndicated investments by venture capital firms: A networking perspective. In *Journal of Business Venturing* 2 (2), pp. 139–154.

Bygrave, William D. (1988): The structure of the investment networks of venture capital firms. In *Journal of Business Venturing* 3 (2), pp. 137–157.

Carpenter, Robert E.; Petersen, Bruce C. (2002): Is the growth of small firms constrained by internal finance? In *Review of Economics and Statistics* 84 (2), pp. 298–309.

Casamatta, Catherine (2003): Financing and advising: Optimal financial contracts with venture capitalists. In *The Journal of Finance* 58 (5), pp. 2059–2085.

Casamatta, Catherine; Haritchabalet, Carole (2007): Experience, screening and syndication in venture capital investments. In *Journal of Financial Intermediation* 16 (3), pp. 368–398.

Cassar, Gavin (2004): The financing of business start-ups. In *Journal of Business Venturing* 19 (2), pp. 261–283.

Certo, S. Trevis; Busenbark, John R.; Woo, Hyun-soo; Semadeni, Matthew (2016): Sample selection bias and Heckman models in strategic management research. In *Strategic Management Journal* 37 (13), pp. 2639–2657.

Chan, Yuk-Shee (1983): On the positive role of financial intermediation in allocation of venture capital in a market with imperfect information. In *The Journal of Finance* 38 (5), pp. 1543–1568.

Chapman, Lizette (2018): Mary Meeker ditches Kleiner Perkins to start her own firm. In *Bloomberg*. Available at: https://www.bloomberg.com/news/articles/2018-09-14/mary-meeker-ditches-kleiner-perkins-to-start-her-own-firm, accessed 7/2/2019.

Chemmanur, Thomas J.; Krishnan, Karthik; Nandy, Debarshi K. (2011): How does venture capital financing improve efficiency in private firms? A look beneath the surface. In *Review of Financial Studies* 24 (12), pp. 4037–4090.

Chemmanur, Thomas J.; Loutskina, Elena; Tian, Xuan (2014): Corporate venture capital, value creation, and innovation. In *Review of Financial. Studies* 27 (8), pp. 2434–2473.

Cholakova, Magdalena; Clarysse, Bart (2015): Does the possibility to make equity investments in crowdfunding projects crowd out reward-based investments? In *Entrepreneurship Theory and Practice* 39 (1), pp. 145–172.

Chung, Sunghun; Animesh, Animesh; Han, Kunsoo; Pinsonneault, Alain (2014): Firms' social media efforts and firm value: Evidence from Facebook business pages. *SSRN working paper*. Available at: https://papers.ssrn.com/sol3/papers2.cfm?abstract_id=2448510

Colao, J. J. (2012): Fred Wilson and the death of venture capital. In *Forbes*. Available at: https://www.forbes.com/sites/jjcolao/2012/05/08/fred-wilson-and-the-death-of-venture-capital/#26a7696942b1, accessed 6/2/2019.

Colombo, Massimo G.; Franzoni, Chiara; Rossi-Lamastra, Cristina (2015): Internal social capital and the attraction of early contributions in crowdfunding. In *Entrepreneurship Theory and Practice* 39 (1), pp. 75–100.

Colombo, Massimo G.; Grilli, Luca (2010): On growth drivers of high-tech start-ups: Exploring the role of founders' human capital and venture capital. In *Journal of Business Venturing* 25 (6), pp. 610–626.

Colombo, Massimo G.; Murtinu, Samuele (2017): Venture capital investments in Europe and portfolio firms' economic performance: Independent versus corporate investors. In *Journal of Economics & Management Strategy* 26 (1), pp. 35–66.

Cosh, Andy; Cumming, Douglas; Hughes, Alan (2009): Outside entrepreneurial capital. In *The Economic Journal* 119 (540), pp. 1494–1533.

Cressy, Robert (2002): Funding gaps: A symposium. In *The Economic Journal* 112 (477), F1-F16.

Cressy, Robert; Malipiero, Alessandro; Munari, Federico (2014): Does VC fund diversification pay off? An empirical investigation of the effects of VC portfolio diversification on fund performance. In *International Entrepreneurship and Management Journal* 10 (1), pp. 139–163.

Cressy, Robert; Munari, Federico; Malipiero, Alessandro (2007): Playing to their strengths? Evidence that specialization in the private equity industry confers competitive advantage. In *Journal of Corporate Finance* 13 (4), pp. 647–669.

Croce, Annalisa; Guerini, Massimiliano; Ughetto, Elisa (2018): Angel financing and the performance of high-tech start-ups. In *Journal of Small Business Management* 56 (2), pp. 208–228.

Croce, Annalisa; Martí, José; Murtinu, Samuele (2013): The impact of venture capital on the productivity growth of European entrepreneurial firms: 'Screening' or 'value added' effect? In *Journal of Business Venturing* 28 (4), pp. 489–510.

Cumming, Douglas J.; Murtinu, Samuele (2016): On the efficiency of bank-affiliated venture capital. *FMA Conference Paper*. Available at: http://www.fmaconferences.org/Vegas/Papers/dougsamfma.pdf.

Das, Sanjiv R.; Jo, Hoje; Kim, Yongtae (2011): Polishing diamonds in the rough: The sources of syndicated venture performance. In *Journal of Financial Intermediation* 20 (2), pp. 199–230.

Davidsson, Per; Recker, Jan; Briel, Frederik von (2018): External enablement of new venture creation: A framework. In *Academy of Management Perspectives (in press)*.

De Clercq, Dirk; Dimov, Dimo (2004): Explaining venture capital firms' syndication behaviour. A longitudinal study. In *Venture Capital* 6 (4), pp. 243–256.

De Clercq, Dirk; Dimov, Dimo (2008): Internal knowledge development and external knowledge access in venture capital investment performance. In *Journal of Management Studies* 45 (3), pp. 585–612.

De Clercq, Dirk; Goulet, Philip K.; Kumpulainen, Mikko; Mäkelä, Manu (2001): Portfolio investment strategies in the Finnish venture capital industry: A longitudinal study. In *Venture Capital* 3 (1), pp. 41–62.

Denis, David J. (2004): Entrepreneurial finance. An overview of the issues and evidence. In *Journal of Corporate Finance* 10 (2), pp. 301–326.

Dimov, Dimo; de Clercq, Dirk (2006): Venture capital investment strategy and portfolio failure rate: A longitudinal study. In *Entrepreneurship Theory and Practice* 30 (2), pp. 207–223.

Dimov, Dimo; Milanov, Hana (2010): The interplay of need and opportunity in venture capital investment syndication. In *Journal of Business Venturing* 25 (4), pp. 331–348.

Drover, Will; Busenitz, Lowell; Matusik, Sharon; Townsend, David; Anglin, Aaron; Dushnitsky, Gary (2017): A review and road map of entrepreneurial equity financing research: Venture capital, corporate venture capital, angel investment, crowdfunding, and accelerators. In *Journal of Management* 43 (6), pp. 1820–1853.

Dushnitsky, Gary; Fitza, Markus A. (2018): Are we missing the platforms for the crowd? Comparing investment drivers across multiple crowdfunding platforms. In *Journal of Business Venturing Insights* 10, article e00100.

Dushnitsky, Gary; Zunino, Diego (2018). The role of crowdfunding in entrepreneurial finance. In Parhankangas A., Mason C., Landström H. (Eds), *Handbook of Research on Crowdfunding*. Forthcoming. Available at: https://ssrn.com/abstract=3237356.

Dutta, Supradeep; Folta, Timothy B. (2016): A comparison of the effect of angels and venture capitalists on innovation and value creation. In *Journal of Business Venturing* 31 (1), pp. 39–54.

Ewens, Michael; Jones, Charles M.; Rhodes-Kropf, Matthew (2013): The price of diversifiable risk in venture capital and private equity. In *Review of Financial Studies* 26 (8), pp. 1854–1889.

Ewens, Michael; Rhodes-Kropf, Matthew (2015): Is a VC partnership greater than the sum of its partners? In *The Journal of Finance* 70 (3), pp. 1081–1113.

Ferrary, Michel (2010): Syndication of venture capital investment: The art of resource pooling. In *Entrepreneurship Theory and Practice* 34 (5), pp. 885–907.

Ferrary, Michel; Granovetter, Mark (2009): The role of venture capital firms in Silicon Valley's complex innovation network. In *Economy and Society* 38 (2), pp. 326–359.

Finlay, Keith; Magnusson, Leandro M. (2009): Implementing weak-instrument robust tests for a general class of instrumental-variables models. In *Stata Journal* 9 (3), p. 398–421.

Firth, David (1993): Bias reduction of maximum likelihood estimates. In *Biometrika* 80 (1), pp. 27–38.

Fritsch, Michael; Schilder, Dirk (2008): Does venture capital investment really require spatial proximity? An empirical investigation. In *Environment and Planning A* 40 (9), pp. 2114–2131.

Fuller, Wayne A. (1977): Some properties of a modification of the limited information estimator. In *Econometrica* 45 (4), pp. 939–953.

Gavetti, Giovanni; Levinthal, Daniel A.; Rivkin, Jan W. (2005): Strategy making in novel and complex worlds: The power of analogy. In *Strategic Management Journal* 26 (8), pp. 691–712.

Germann, Frank; Ebbes, Peter; Grewal, Rajdeep (2015): The chief marketing officer matters! In *Journal of Marketing* 79 (3), pp. 1–22.

Goldman Sachs (2015): The future of finance – Part 3 – The socialization of finance. Available at: https://www.planet-fintech.com/file/167061/, accessed 5/5/2017.

Gompers, Paul (1995): Optimal investment, monitoring, and the staging of venture capital. In *The Journal of Finance* 50 (5), pp. 1461–1489.

Gompers, Paul; Gornall, William; Kaplan, Steven N.; Strebulaev, Ilya A. (2016a): How do venture capitalists make decisions? National Bureau of Economic Research NBER Working Paper No. 22587

Gompers, Paul; Kovner, Anna; Lerner, Josh (2009): Specialization and success. Evidence from venture capital. In *Journal of Economics & Management Strategy* 18 (3), pp. 817–844.

Gompers, Paul; Lerner, Josh (2001): The venture capital revolution. In *Journal of Economic Perspectives* 15 (2), pp. 145–168.

Gompers, Paul; Lerner, Josh (2004): *The Venture Capital Cycle*. MIT Press.

Gompers, Paul; Mukharlyamov, Vladimir; Xuan, Yuhai (2016b): The cost of friendship. In *Journal of Financial Economics* 119 (3), pp. 626–644.

Gorman, Michael; Sahlman, William A. (1989): What do venture capitalists do? In *Journal of Business Venturing* 4 (4), pp. 231–248.

Grilli, Luca; Murtinu, Samuele (2014): Government, venture capital and the growth of European high-tech entrepreneurial firms. In *Research Policy* 43 (9), pp. 1523–1543.

Guerini, Massimiliano; Quas, Anita (2016): Governmental venture capital in Europe: Screening and certification. In *Journal of Business Venturing* 31 (2), pp. 175–195.

Gupta, Anil K.; Sapienza, Harry J. (1992): Determinants of venture capital firms' preferences regarding the industry diversity and geographic scope of their investments. In *Journal of Business Venturing* 7 (5), pp. 347–362.

Hall, Bronwyn H.; Lerner, Josh (2010): The financing of R&D and innovation. In *Handbook of the Economics of Innovation*, vol. 1. Elsevier, pp. 609–639.

Hamilton, Barton H.; Nickerson, Jackson A. (2003): Correcting for endogeneity in strategic management research. In *Strategic Organization* 1 (1), pp. 51–78.

Hansen, Lars Peter; Heaton, John; Yaron, Amir (1996): Finite-sample properties of some alternative GMM estimators. In *Journal of Business & Economic Statistics* 14 (3), p. 262–280.

Hautz, Julia; Seidl, David; Whittington, Richard (2017): Open strategy: Dimensions, dilemmas, dynamics. In *Long Range Planning* 50 (3), pp. 298–309.

Heckman, James (1974): Shadow prices, market wages, and labor supply. In *Econometrica* 42 (4), pp. 679–694.

Heckman, James (1979): Sample selection bias as a specification error. In *Econometrica* 47 (1), pp. 153–161.

Hege, Ulrich; Palomino, Frédéric; Schwienbacher, Armin (2009): Venture capital performance: The disparity between Europe and the United States. In *Finance* 30 (1), pp. 7–50.

Hellmann, Thomas; Puri Manju (2002): Venture capital and the professionalization of start-up firms. Empirical evidence. In *The Journal of Finance* 57 (1), pp. 169–197.

Hochberg, Yael V.; Lindsey, Laura A.; Westerfield, Mark M. (2015): Resource accumulation through economic ties: Evidence from venture capital. In *Journal of Financial Economics* 118 (2), pp. 245–267.

Hochberg, Yael V.; Ljungqvist, Alexander; Lu, Yang (2007): Whom you know matters: Venture capital networks and investment performance. In *The Journal of Finance* 62 (1), pp. 251–301.

Hoetker, Glenn (2007): The use of logit and probit models in strategic management research: Critical issues. In *Strategic Management Journal* 28 (4), pp. 331–343.

Homburg, Christian; Hahn, Alexander; Bornemann, Torsten; Sandner, Philipp (2014): The role of chief marketing officers for venture capital funding: Endowing new ventures with marketing legitimacy. In *Journal of Marketing Research* 51 (5), pp. 625–644.

Hopp, Christian (2010): When do venture capitalists collaborate? Evidence on the driving forces of venture capital syndication. In *Small Business Economics* 35 (4), pp. 417–431.

Hopp, Christian; Lukas, Christian (2014): A signaling perspective on partner selection in venture capital syndicates. In *Entrepreneurship Theory and Practice* 38 (3), pp. 635–670.

Hopp, Christian; Rieder, Finn (2005): Empirical evidence on the syndication of venture capital and shared real option ownership. *University of Konstanz and Bundesverband Deutscher Banken working paper*. Available at: http://cite-seerx.ist.psu.edu/viewdoc/download?doi=10.1.1.527.3782&rep=rep1&type=pdf

Hornuf, Lars; Schmitt, Matthias; Stenzhorn, Eliza (2018): Equity crowdfunding in Germany and the UK: Follow-up funding and firm failure. *Max Planck Institute for Innovation & Competition Research Paper* No. 17–09; *CESifo Working Paper Series* No. 6642. Available at: https://ssrn.com/abstract=3020820

Hornuf, Lars; Schwienbacher, Armin (2014): Crowdinvesting – Angel investing for the masses? In *Handbook of Research on Venture Capital*, vol. 3, Business Angels, Forthcoming. Available at: https://ssrn.com/abstract=2401515

Hornuf, Lars; Schwienbacher, Armin (2016): Should securities regulation promote equity crowdfunding? *SSRN working paper*. Available at: https://ssrn.com/abstract=2412124

Hsu, David H. (2004): What do entrepreneurs pay for venture capital affiliation? In *The Journal of Finance* 59 (4), pp. 1805–1844.

Hsu, David H. (2006): Venture capitalists and cooperative start-up commercialization strategy. In *Management Science* 52 (2), pp. 204–219.

Huhman, Heather (2012): Crowdfunding comes to small businesses. In *Business Insider* Available at: http://www.businessinsider.com/crowdfunding-comes-to-small-businesses-2012-6, accessed 27/3/2017.

Humphery-Jenner, Mark (2012): Private equity fund size, investment size, and value creation. In *Review of Finance* 16 (3), pp. 799–835.

Humphery-Jenner, Mark (2013): Diversification in private equity funds: On knowledge sharing, risk aversion, and limited attention. In *Journal of Financial and Quantitative Analysis* 48 (05), pp. 1545–1572.

Hurley, James (2011): Crowdcube brings angel investing to the masses. In *Telegraph*. Available at: http://www.telegraph.co.uk/finance/businessclub/8324129/Crowdcube-brings-angel-investing-to-the-masses.html, accessed 27/3/2017.

Ireland, R. Duane; Hitt, Michael A.; Sirmon, David G. (2003): A model of strategic entrepreneurship: The construct and its dimensions. In *Journal of Management* 29 (6), pp. 963–989.

Jääskeläinen, Mikko (2012): Venture capital syndication: Synthesis and future directions. In *International Journal of Management Reviews* 14 (4), pp. 444–463.

Jääskeläinen, Mikko; Maula, Markku; Seppä, Tuukka (2006): Allocation of attention to portfolio companies and the performance of venture capital firms. In *Entrepreneurship Theory and Practice* 30 (2), pp. 185–206.

Jensen, Michael C.; Meckling, William H. (1976): Theory of the firm: Managerial behavior, agency costs and ownership structure. In *Journal of Financial Economics* 3 (4), pp. 305–360.

Kaiser, Dieter G.; Lauterbach, Rainer (2007): The need for diversification and its impact on the syndication probability of venture capital investments. In *The Journal of Alternative Investments* 10 (3), p. 62–79.

Kaminski, Jermain; Hopp, Christian; Tykvová, Tereza (2019): New technology assessment in entrepreneurial financing – Does crowdfunding predict venture capital investments? In *Technological Forecasting and Social Change* 139, pp. 287–302.

Kaplan, Steven N.; Strömberg, Per (2003): Financial contracting theory meets the real world: An empirical analysis of venture capital contracts. In *Review of Economic Studies* 70 (2), pp. 281–315.

Katila, Riitta; Rosenberger, Jeff D.; Eisenhardt, Kathleen M. (2008): Swimming with sharks: Technology ventures, defense mechanisms and corporate relationships. In *Administrative Science Quarterly* 53 (2), pp. 295–332.

Kelly, Roger (2011): The performance and prospects of European venture capital. *EIF Working Paper*, No. 2011/09. Available at: http://www.eif.org/news_centre/publications/EIF_Working_Paper_2011_009.htm, accessed 3/3/2019.

Kerr, William R.; Lerner, Josh; Schoar, Antoinette (2014): The consequences of entrepreneurial finance: Evidence from angel financings. In *Review of Financial Studies* 27 (1), pp. 20–55.

Kirsch, David; Goldfarb, Brent; Gera, Azi (2009): Form or substance: The role of business plans in venture capital decision making. In *Strategic Management Journal* 30 (5), pp. 487–515.

Klöhn, Lars; Hornuf, Lars; Schilling, Tobias (2016): The regulation of crowdfunding in the German small investor protection act: Content, consequences, critique, suggestions. In *European Company Law* 13 (2), pp. 56–66.

Knill, April (2009): Should venture capitalists put all their eggs in one basket? Diversification versus pure-play strategies in venture capital. In *Financial Management* 38 (3), pp. 441–486.

Kortum, Samuel; Lerner, Josh (2000): Assessing the contribution of venture capital to innovation. In *The RAND Journal of Economics* 31 (4), p. 674–692.

Krishnan, C. N. V.; Ivanov, Vladimir I.; Masulis, Ronald W.; Singh, Ajai K. (2011): Venture capital reputation, post-IPO performance, and corporate governance. In *Journal of Financial and Quantitative Analysis* 46 (5), pp. 1295–1333.

Kumar, V.; Bhaskaran, Vikram; Mirchandani, Rohan; Shah, Milap (2013): Practice prize winner – creating a measurable social media marketing strategy. Increasing the value and ROI of intangibles and tangibles for hokey pokey. In *Marketing Science* 32 (2), pp. 194–212.

Kuppuswamy, Venkat; Bayus, Barry L. (2017): Does my contribution to your crowdfunding project matter? In *Journal of Business Venturing* 32 (1), pp. 72–89.

Lerner, Josh (1994): The syndication of venture capital investments. In *Financial Management*, Vol. 23 (3), pp. 16–27.

Lerner, Josh (1995): Venture capitalists and the oversight of private firms. In *The Journal of Finance* 50 (1), pp. 301–318.

Lin, Yan; Boh, Wai Fong; Goh, Kim Huat (2014): How different are crowdfunders? Examining archetypes of crowdfunders and their choice of projects. In *Academy of Management Proceedings* 2014 (1), ID13309.

Lockett, Andy; Wright, Mike (1999): The syndication of private equity: Evidence from the UK. In *Venture Capital* 1 (4), pp. 303–324.

Lockett, Andy; Wright, Mike (2001): The syndication of venture capital investments. In *Omega* 29 (5), pp. 375–390.

Lukkarinen, Anna; Teich, Jeffrey E.; Wallenius, Hannele; Wallenius, Jyrki (2016): Success drivers of online equity crowdfunding campaigns. In *Decision Support Systems* 87, pp. 26–38.

Lungeanu, R.; Zajac, E. J. (2016): Venture capital ownership as a contingent resource: How owner-firm fit influences IPO outcomes. In *Academy of Management Journal* 59 (3), pp. 930–955.

Macmillan, Ian C.; Zemann, Lauriann; Subbanarasimha, P. N. (1987): Criteria distinguishing successful from unsuccessful ventures in the venture screening process. In *Journal of Business Venturing* 2 (2), pp. 123–137.

Manigart, Sophie; Lockett, Andy; Meuleman, Miguel; Wright, Mike; Landstrom, Hans; Bruining, Hans; Desbrières, Philippe; Hommel, Ulrich(2006): Venture capitalists' decision to syndicate. In *Entrepreneurship Theory and Practice* 30 (2), pp. 131–153.

Manigart, Sophie; Wright, Mike (2013): Venture capital investors and portfolio firms. In *Foundations and Trends in Entrepreneurship* 9 (5), pp. 365–570.

Manning, Stephan; Bejarano, Thomas A. (2017): Convincing the crowd: Entrepreneurial storytelling in crowdfunding campaigns. In *Strategic Organization* 15 (2), pp. 194–219.

Markowitz, Harry (1952): Portfolio selection. In *The Journal of Finance* 7 (1), pp. 77–91.

Matusik, Sharon F.; Fitza, Markus A. (2012): Diversification in the venture capital industry. Leveraging knowledge under uncertainty. In *Strategic Management Journal* 33 (4), pp. 407–426.

Matzler, Kurt (Ed.) (2014): *Strategie und Leadership. Festschrift für Hans H. Hinterhuber*. Wiesbaden: Springer Gabler.

Meuleman, Miguel; Amess, Kevin; Wright, Mike; Scholes, Louise (2009): Agency, strategic entrepreneurship, and the performance of private equity-backed buyouts. In *Entrepreneurship Theory and Practice* 33 (1), pp. 213–239.

Milanov, Hana; Shepherd, Dean A. (2013): The importance of the first relationship: The ongoing influence of initial network on future status. In *Strategic Management Journal* 34 (6), pp. 727–750.

Mitchell, Falconer; Reid, Gavin C.; Terry, Nicholas G. (1997): Venture capital supply and accounting information system development. In *Entrepreneurship Theory and Practice* 21 (4), pp. 45–62.

Mollick, Ethan (2014): The dynamics of crowdfunding. An exploratory study. In *Journal of Business Venturing* 29 (1), pp. 1–16.

Mollick, Ethan; Kuppuswamy, Venkat (2014), After the campaign: Outcomes of crowdfunding. *UNC Kenan-Flagler Research Paper* No. 2376997. Available at: https://ssrn.com/abstract=2376997.

Mollick, Ethan; Nanda, Ramana (2016): Wisdom or madness? Comparing crowds with expert evaluation in funding the arts. In *Management Science* 62 (6), pp. 1533–1553.

Moreira, Marcelo J. (2003): A conditional likelihood ratio test for structural models. In *Econometrica* 71 (4), pp. 1027–1048.

Moss, Todd W.; Neubaum, Donald O.; Meyskens, Moriah (2015): The effect of virtuous and entrepreneurial orientations on microfinance lending and repayment: A signaling theory perspective. In *Entrepreneurship Theory and Practice* 39 (1), pp. 27–52.

Murray, Michael P. (2006): Avoiding invalid instruments and coping with weak instruments. In *The Journal of Economic Perspectives* 20 (4), pp. 111–132.

Nicholls-Nixon, Charlene L.; Cooper, Arnold C.; Woo, Carolyn Y. (2000): Strategic experimentation: Understanding change and performance in new ventures. In *Journal of Business Venturing* 15 (5–6), pp. 493–521.

Norton, Edgar; Tenenbaum, Bernard H. (1993): Specialization versus diversification as a venture capital investment strategy. In *Journal of Business Venturing* 8 (5), pp. 431–442.

Norton, Edward; Wang, Hua; Ai, Chunrong (2004): Computing interaction effects and standard errors in logit and probit models. In *Stata Journal* 4, pp. 154–167.

O'Brien, Robert M. (2007): A caution regarding rules of thumb for variance inflation factors. In *Quality & Quantity* 41 (5), pp. 673–690.

Pahnke, E.; McDonald, R.; Wang, D.; Hallen, B. (2015): Exposed: Venture capital, competitor ties, and entrepreneurial innovation. In *Academy of Management Journal* 58 (5), pp. 1334–1360.

Park, Haemin Dennis; Steensma, H. Kevin (2012): When does corporate venture capital add value for new ventures? In *Strategic Management Journal* 33 (1), pp. 1–22.

Petty, Jeffrey S.; Gruber, Marc (2011): 'In pursuit of the real deal': A longitudinal study of VC decision making. In *Journal of Business Venturing* 26 (2), pp. 172–188.

Pisani, Bob (2016): Equity crowdfunding coming soon for average investors. In *CNBC*. Available online at: http://www.cnbc.com/2016/05/12/equity-crowdfunding-coming-soon-for-average-investors.html, accessed 5/5/2017.

Plummer, L. A.; Allison, T. H.; Connelly, B. L. (2016): Better together? Signaling interactions in new venture pursuit of initial external capital. In *Academy of Management Journal* 59 (5), pp. 1585–1604.

Puri, Manju; Zarutskie, Rebecca (2012): On the life cycle dynamics of venture-capital- and non-venture-capital-financed firms. In *The Journal of Finance* 67 (6), pp. 2247–2293.

Ralcheva, Aleksandrina; Roosenboom, Peter (2016): On the road to success in equity crowdfunding. Working paper. Available at: https://ssrn.com/abstract=2727742

Rishika, Rishika; Kumar, Ashish; Janakiraman, Ramkumar; Bezawada, Ram (2013): The effect of customers' social media participation on customer visit frequency and profitability: An empirical investigation. In *Information Systems Research* 24 (1), pp. 108–127.

Roodman, David (2006): How to do xtabond2: An introduction to 'difference' and 'system' GMM in Stata. In *Center for Global Development Working Papers* (103). Available at: http://citeseerx.ist.psu.edu/viewdoc/download?doi=10.1.1.612.3134&rep=rep1&type=pdf

Roodman, David (2009): A note on the theme of too many instruments. In *Oxford Bulletin of Economics and Statistics* 71 (1), pp. 135–158.

Saboo, Alok R.; Chakravarty, Anindita; Grewal, Rajdeep (2016): Organizational debut on the public stage: Marketing myopia and initial public offerings. In *Marketing Science* 35 (4), pp. 656–675.

Sahlman, William A. (1990): The structure and governance of venture-capital organizations. In *Journal of Financial Economics* 27 (2), pp. 473–521.

Sailer, Anna-Sophie; Schlagwein, Daniel; Schoder, Detlef (2017): Open strategy: State of the art review and research agenda. *Conference paper, 38th International Conference on Information Systems.*

Samila, Sampsa; Sorenson, Olav (2010): Venture capital, entrepreneurship, and economic growth. In *The Review of Economics and Statistics* 93 (1), pp. 338–349.

Sapienza, Harry J.; Manigart, Sophie; Vermeir, Wim (1996): Venture capitalist governance and value added in four countries. In *Journal of Business Venturing* 11 (6), pp. 439–469.

Schlagwein, Daniel; Bjørn-Andersen, Niels (2014): Organizational learning with crowdsourcing: The revelatory case of LEGO. In *Journal of the Association for Information Systems* 15 (11), pp. 754–778.

Schwienbacher, Armin (2008): Venture capital investment practices in Europe and the United States. In *Financial Markets and Portfolio Management* 22 (3), pp. 195–217.

Schwienbacher, Armin (2013): The entrepreneur's investor choice. The impact on later-stage firm development. In *Journal of Business Venturing* 28 (4), pp. 528–545.

Schwienbacher, Armin; Larralde, Benjamin (2010): Crowdfunding of small entrepreneurial ventures. *Handbook of Entrepreneurial Finance*, Oxford University Press, Forthcoming. Available at: https://ssrn.com/abstract=1699183

Sequoia (2019): The Dentmakers. Available at: https://www.sequoiacap.com/companies/, accessed 7/2/2019.

Signori, Andrea; Vismara, Silvio (2018): Does success bring success? The post-offering lives of equity-crowdfunded firms. In *Journal of Corporate Finance* 50, pp. 575–591.

Sørensen, Morten (2007): How smart is smart money? A two-sided matching model of venture capital. In *The Journal of Finance* 62 (6), pp. 2725–2762.

Sorenson, Olav; Stuart, Toby E. (2001): Syndication networks and the spatial distribution of venture capital investments. In *American Journal of Sociology* 106 (6), pp. 1546–1588.

Stanko, Michael A.; Henard, David H. (2017): Toward a better understanding of crowdfunding, openness and the consequences for innovation. In *Research Policy* 46 (4), pp. 784–798.

Stock, James; Yogo, Motohiro (2005): Testing for weak instruments in linear IV regression. In Donald W. K. Andrews (Ed.), *Identification and Inference for Econometric Models*. New York: Cambridge University Press, pp. 80–108.

Stock, James; Yogo, Motohiro; Wright, J. (2002): A survey of weak instruments and weak identification in generalized method of moments. In *Journal of Business and Economic Statistics* 20, pp. 518–529.

Tavakoli, Asin; Schlagwein, Daniel; Schoder, Detlef (2017): Open strategy. Literature review, re-analysis of cases and conceptualisation as a practice. In *The Journal of Strategic Information Systems* 26 (3), pp. 163–184.

Ter Wal, Anne L. J.; Alexy, Oliver; Block, Jörn; Sandner, Philipp G. (2016): The best of both worlds: The benefits of open-specialized and closed-diverse syndication networks for new ventures' success. In *Administrative Science Quarterly* 61 (3), pp. 393–432.

The Economist (2012): The new thundering herd. Available at: https://www.economist.com/business/2012/06/16/the-new-thundering-herd, accessed 6/2/2019.

Thorngate, Warren (1976): 'In general' vs. 'it depends': Some comments of the Gergen-Schlenker debate. In *Personality and Social Psychology Bulletin* 2 (4), pp. 404–410.

Tian, Xuan (2012): The role of venture capital syndication in value creation for entrepreneurial firms. In *Review of Finance* 16 (1), pp. 245–283.

Timmons, Jeffry A.; Bygrave, William D. (1986): Venture capital's role in financing innovation for economic growth. In *Journal of Business Venturing* 1 (2), pp. 161–176.

Tucker, Jennifer Wu (2010): Selection bias and econometric remedies in accounting and finance research. In *Journal of Accounting Literature* 29, p. 31–57.

Tyebjee, Tyzoon T.; Bruno, Albert V. (1984): A model of venture capitalist investment activity. In *Management Science* 30 (9), pp. 1051–1066.

Tykvová, Tereza (2018): Venture capital and private equity financing: An overview of recent literature and an agenda for future research. In *Journal of Business Economics* 88 (3–4), pp. 325–362.

Ueda, Masako (2004): Banks versus venture capital: Project evaluation, screening, and expropriation. In *The Journal of Finance* 59 (2), pp. 601–621.

Vismara, Silvio (2016): Equity retention and social network theory in equity crowdfunding. In *Small Business Economics* 46 (4), pp. 579–590.

Vulkan, Nir; Åstebro, Thomas; Sierra, Manuel Fernandez (2016): Equity crowdfunding. A new phenomena. In *Journal of Business Venturing Insights* 5, pp. 37–49.

Wang, Lanfang; Wang, Susheng (2012): Economic freedom and cross-border venture capital performance. In *Journal of Empirical Finance* 19 (1), pp. 26–50.

Werth, Jochen Christian; Boeert, Patrick (2013): Co-investment networks of business angels and the performance of their start-up investments. In *IJEV* 5 (3), p. 240–256.

Windmeijer, Frank (2005): A finite sample correction for the variance of linear efficient two-step GMM estimators. In *Journal of Econometrics* 126 (1), pp. 25–51.

Wooldridge, Jeffrey M. (2009): *Introductory Econometrics. A Modern Approach*. 4th ed. Mason OH: South Western Cengage Learning.

Wright, Mike; Lockett, Andy (2003): The structure and management of alliances: Syndication in the venture capital industry. In *Journal of Management Studies* 40 (8), pp. 2073–2102.

8. Appendix

Abstract

This dissertation investigates deal selection and investor value-added in venture capital (VC) financing and equity crowdfunding. Its empirical analyses provide novel evidence on the value-added of equity crowdfunding investors and explain the deal selection, syndication and value-added of VC investors in a greater level of detail than previous research.

Entrepreneurial equity investors, such as VC investors and equity crowdfunders, play an important role in the start-up ecosystem, as they provide much-needed capital to entrepreneurial ventures which often face challenges in obtaining adequate funding. However, the fundamental question of entrepreneurial equity investors' influence on their portfolio companies has not yet been answered conclusively. Since the funding of entrepreneurial ventures is characterised by a high level of information asymmetries and uncertainty, VC investors have adopted a set of typical measures throughout their investment process. These measures include an extensive deal selection process with an extremely low acceptance rate, risk-reducing contracting and deal-structuring measures, and an active post-investment involvement. Given that VC investors routinely combine these measures when investing in companies, it is very challenging for empirical research to isolate selection and treatment effects and draw conclusions on investors' effect on portfolio companies. Consequently, it has long been disputed whether the observed superior performance of venture capital-backed companies is caused by venture capitalists' post-investment involvement or rather reflects the fact that VC investors select companies with a higher potential for success in the first place. However, recent research has started to disentangle selection and value-adding effects, and provides evidence suggesting that the superior performance of VC-backed companies is at least partially caused by the value-adding contributions of VC investors. Besides that, there is mixed evidence as to whether VC investors select companies with greater inherent development potential.

Two important aspects of the research on deal selection and investor value-added continue to attract further scholarly attention. First, current research attempts to understand differences in the value-adding contributions and performance implications of the various investor types and funding models that have recently emerged as significant alternatives to traditional VC financing. Second, since the extant literature on selection and treatment in venture capital is typically limited to simplistic comparisons of different types of VC investors, scholars have called for a more nuanced understanding of potential heterogeneity among VC investors with respect to deal selection and investor value-added.

This dissertation aims to contribute to this academic discourse by answering three research questions. Research Question 1 deals with broadening the literature on investor value-added to equity crowdfunding: *How does equity crowdfunding investors' value-added to portfolio companies compare to traditional early-stage investors' value-added?* Research Question 2 aims at providing a more nuanced understanding of selection and treatment effects in VC financing that accounts for heterogeneity among investors by evaluating venture capitalists' industry specialisation as an antecedent for potentially superior investment selection and value-added: *How does venture capitalists' industry specialisation affect their ability to select high-potential ventures and add value to them?* Research Question 3 aims at establishing a more granular understanding of VC investors' syndication practices, which are closely related to their deal selection, by evaluating the influence of investors' industry specialisation on syndication: *How does venture capitalists' industry specialisation affect the formation and composition of syndicates?*

All three research questions are assessed through dedicated empirical analyses using large-scale secondary datasets and advanced empirical methodologies. The first essay employs an international sample of equity-crowdfunded companies and matched peers that received angel or seed funding to address Research Question 1. The identification strategy rests on a rigid matching procedure and instrumental variables (IV) regressions that address endogeneity. Moreover, the analyses on investor value-added account for several performance dimensions to obtain a fine-grained understanding of the alleged differences. The results of the essay reveal that equity-crowdfunded companies' subsequent performance is causally negatively affected compared to peers using traditional entrepreneurial equity financing, since equity crowdfunders add less value to portfolio companies than venture capitalists and business angels. The findings are consistent with the explanation that equity crowdfunders' value-added is hampered by a combination of suboptimal monitoring, a more complex investor–company relationship – that currently fails to make use of crowd investors' potentially valuable managerial and social capital resources – as well as inferior reputation.

166

To answer Research Question 2, the analyses in the second essay draw on a unique longitudinal dataset on European venture financing and start-up performance (VICO 4.0) and employ advanced empirical methods, including the two-step system generalised method of moments estimator (GMM-SYS) that accounts for the endogenous nature of VC financing. This research extends the scientific knowledge on venture capitalists' investment selection and value-added by providing evidence for heterogeneity among investors in their ability to select promising ventures and add value to them. The analyses show that high levels of industry specialisation are detrimental to investors' value-added, suggesting that venture capitalists benefit from diverse experience rather than deep industry knowledge in their portfolio work. Moreover, the findings are consistent with the argument that greater investor–company-fit may impair investor value-added due to the risk of knowledge appropriation and information leakage. However, the results of the second essay also indicate that there is heterogeneity among VC investors in their ability to select ventures with greater inherent growth potential in the sense that greater specialisation and investor–company-fit positively affect venture capitalists' ability to select high-potential companies.

The third essay draws on the VICO 4.0 dataset, too, and uses tailored estimation techniques, including GMM-SYS and a rare events logistics model analysing both realised and unrealised lead investor–co-investor dyads to tackle Research Question 3. It provides an integrated perspective on lead investors' decision to form a syndicate as well as their choice of co-investors against the background of VC investors' investor–company-fit. The analyses show that the higher the lead VC investors' fit with the focal company, the less likely they are to syndicate a deal. However, conditional on the decision to syndicate, the lead investor is more likely to choose to syndicate with co-investors who have a higher fit with the focal venture. This empirical finding is thus consistent with theoretical arguments suggesting that specialised expertise is an important resource that reduces information asymmetries and therefore allows investors to make better informed investment decisions. Moreover, this finding highlights that investors form syndicates in an opportunistic manner, and it provides additional evidence for the notion that VC investors seek to acquire complementary resources when syndicating.

Taken together, this dissertation makes several theoretical contributions to the entrepreneurial equity financing literature as well as adjacent research areas. First and foremost, the analyses advance the literature stream on investment selection and investor value-added in entrepreneurial equity financing in both breadth and depth. The research broadens the scholarly understanding of investor value-added, hitherto spanning VC and business angel (BA) financing, to equity crowdfunding, which is an increasingly important funding mechanism for start-ups whose effect on companies has hitherto been underexplored. Moreover, the second essay deepens the scientific knowledge on venture capitalists' screening and value-added by providing novel evidence for heterogeneity among investors in their ability to select promising ventures and add value to them. Thereby, the essay advances this literature stream, which currently lacks a granular understanding of VC investor characteristics affecting selection and treatment effects. In addition, this dissertation also contributes to the literature stream on VC specialisation by alluding to the influence of industry specialisation on outcomes across different stages of the investment process – ranging from deal selection and deal structuring to the post-investment value-added. Similarly, this dissertation also advances the literature stream on VC syndication by providing a novel, integrated perspective on lead investors' decision to form a syndicate and their choice of co-investors. Further, certain aspects of this research are relevant for other research streams of the management literature, outside the area of entrepreneurial finance, too. For instance, the results that delineate how VC investors can acquire relevant deal selection and value-adding capabilities through industry specialisation inform the literature on organisational learning. Also, the findings on equity crowdfunding link the research stream on crowdfunding with the literature on open strategy and innovation and thus contribute to uniting these research fields. In the broader context of management research, the findings of this dissertation add to the resource-based view as they identify specific resources that are valuable in the context of entrepreneurial finance. Besides that, the essay on equity crowdfunding also puts agency cost theory into the context of new digital funding models, and thus validates the theory's ongoing relevance in the digital age.

Finally, this research offers several practical implications for different actors in the entrepreneurial finance space. First, this research informs regulators, entrepreneurs and operators of equity crowdfunding platforms of the current drawbacks of equity crowdfunding. In its current pre-mature state, equity crowdfunding is unfortunately no panacea for the scarcity of entrepreneurial risk capital, and platform providers and regulators need to make changes to establish it as an adequate funding alternative for entrepreneurs. Second, this dissertation offers an important, empirically-backed takeaway for VC investors. Specifically, the results from the second essay suggest that VC investors face a trade-off: between acquiring strong industry specialisation that helps them select high-potential companies, and diverse experience that is beneficial for their value-added. Thus, VC fund managers need to steer towards an optimal level of diversification so as to strike a balance between investment selection and value-added to maximise fund returns given these boundary conditions. The results of this research further underscore that syndication can be an effective means for venture capitalists to acquire complementary capabilities, and syndication can therefore be an effective way to manage the trade-off between investment selection and value-added. Of course, this trade-off may lead to conflicts of interests with entrepreneurs that seek to benefit from investors' value-adding contributions, and these research findings are therefore valuable for entrepreneurs, too. Moreover, these findings enable more specific interventions by regulators and policymakers, as these actors should be interested in fostering investor value-added rather than cherry-picking by VC investors.

In summary, this dissertation underscores entrepreneurial equity investors' significant influence on portfolio companies and fosters a more nuanced understanding of selection and value-added effects in VC financing by delineating heterogeneity among investors – which should thus be accounted for by future research delving into VC investors' investment decisions and portfolio work.

Abstract – German Version

Diese Dissertation untersucht die Investitionsauswahl und Wertstiftung von Venture-Capital- (VC) und Equity-Crowdfunding-Investoren. Die empirischen Analysen liefern neue Erkenntnisse zur Wertstiftung von Equity-Crowdfunding-Investoren und erklären die Investitionsauswahl, -syndizierung und Wertstiftung von VC-Investoren in einem höheren Detailgrad als frühere Untersuchungen.

Risikokapitalgeber spielen eine wichtige Rolle für das Innovations-Ökosystem, da sie das dringend benötigte Kapital für Jungunternehmen bereitstellen, die strukturelle Schwierigkeiten haben, eine angemessene Finanzierung zu erhalten. Die Grundsatzfrage nach dem Einfluss, den Risikokapitalgeber auf ihre Portfoliounternehmen haben (oder nicht haben), ist jedoch bisher nicht abschließend beantwortet. Da die Finanzierung von Jungunternehmen durch ein hohes Maß an Informationsasymmetrien und Unsicherheit gekennzeichnet ist, wenden VC-Investoren im Rahmen ihres Investitionsprozesses eine Reihe typischer Vorsichtsmaßnahmen an. Diese reichen von einem umfangreichen Auswahlprozess, an dessen Ende nur extrem wenige der evaluierten Investitionen getätigt werden, über risikoreduzierende Vertrags- und Investitions-Strukturierungsmaßnahmen bis hin zu einem aktiven Mitwirken der Investoren an der Unternehmensführung ihrer Portfoliofirmen. Da VC-Investoren diese Maßnahmen bei Investitionen in Unternehmen in der Regel kombinieren, ist es seit langem umstritten und empirisch schwer nachzuweisen, ob VC-Investoren bei Ihren Portfolio-Unternehmen durch ihr Mitwirken einen Mehrwert stiften oder ob der vergleichsweise größere unternehmerische Erfolg VC-finanzierter Firmen dadurch zu erklären ist, dass VC-Investoren Unternehmen mit höherem Erfolgspotenzial auswählen. Neuere Forschungsbeiträge haben jedoch damit begonnen, kausale Effekte zu isolieren und liefern Hinweise darauf, dass der überdurchschnittliche Erfolg von VC-finanzierten Unternehmen zumindest teilweise durch die Wertstiftungsbeiträge von VC-Investoren verursacht wird. Darüber hinaus liefert die neuere Forschung gemischte Erkenntnisse zur Frage, ob VC-Investoren dazu in der Lage sind, Unternehmen mit einem größeren inhärenten Entwicklungspotenzial auszuwählen.

Zwei wesentliche Aspekte des Forschungsfeldes zu Investitionsauswahl und Wertstiftung von Risikokapitalgebern ziehen jedoch weiterhin die Aufmerksamkeit der Forschergemeinde auf sich. Einerseits bieten neue Investorentypen und Finanzierungsmodelle, die sich als relevante Alternativen zur traditionellen VC-Finanzierung etabliert haben, neue Untersuchungsansätze. Hierbei gilt es, die verschiedenen Investorentypen und Finanzierungsmodelle hinsichtlich ihrer Wertstiftungsbeiträge und möglicher Leistungsauswirkungen für Portfoliounternehmen zu untersuchen. Zum anderen wird ein nuancierteres Verständnis der potenziellen Heterogenität von VC-Investoren hinsichtlich Investitionsauswahl und Wertstiftung gefordert. Solche Untersuchungen sind von Wert, da sich die vorhandene Literatur zur Investitionsauswahl und Wertstiftung von Risikokapitalgebern typischerweise auf vereinfachte Vergleiche verschiedener Archetypen von VC-Investoren beschränkt.

Diese Dissertation zielt darauf ab, zu diesem akademischen Diskurs beizutragen, indem sie drei Forschungsfragen beantwortet. Forschungsfrage 1 dient der Ausweitung der Forschung zur Wertstiftung von Risikokapitalgebern auf Equity-Crowdfunding-Investoren: *Wie unterscheiden sich Equity-Crowdfunding-Investoren und traditionelle Risikokapitalgeber hinsichtlich ihrer Wertstiftung für Portfoliounternehmen?* Forschungsfrage 2 dient dazu, ein differenzierteres Verständnis der Selektions- und Wertstiftungseffekte von VC-Investoren zu erzielen, indem die Branchenspezialisierung von VC-Investoren als Ursache für eine möglicherweise überlegene Investitionsauswahl und Wertstiftung untersucht wird: *Wie wirkt sich die Branchenspezialisierung von VC-Investoren auf deren Fähigkeiten aus, potenzialstarke Unternehmen auszuwählen und Mehrwert für diese Unternehmen zu stiften?* Forschungsfrage 3 zielt darauf ab, ein detaillierteres Verständnis der Syndizierungspraktiken, die integraler Bestandteil der Investitionsauswahl sind, zu schaffen, indem der Einfluss der Branchenspezialisierung von Investoren auf Syndizierungspraktiken untersucht wird: *Welchen Einfluss hat die Branchenspezialisierung von VC-Investoren auf die Bildung und Zusammensetzung von Investitionssyndikaten?*

Alle drei Forschungsfragen werden durch empirische Analysen unter Verwendung groß angelegter Sekundärdatensätze und fortschrittlicher Methoden untersucht. Die erste Untersuchung fußt auf einer internationalen Stichprobe von Unternehmen, die Equity-Crowdfunding nutzen sowie zugehörigen Vergleichsunternehmen, die stattdessen eine traditionelle VC- oder Business-Angel-Finanzierung erhalten haben. Für die empirische Analyse wird eine strenge, mehrstufige Auswahl der Vergleichsunternehmen vorgenommen und eine Instrumentvariablenschätzung angewandt, um einem Einfluss von Endogenität auf die Untersuchungsergebnisse zu begegnen. Darüber hinaus verwendet die Untersuchung verschiedene Kenngrößen für den Unternehmenserfolg, um ein differenziertes Bild der möglichen Unterschiede zu gewinnen. Die Ergebnisse zeigen, dass Unternehmen, die eine Equity-Crowdfunding-Finanzierung nutzen, in der Folge einen geringeren unternehmerischen Erfolg erzielen als vergleichbare Unternehmen, die auf eine traditionelle Finanzierung durch VC-Investoren oder Business Angels zurückgreifen. Die Ergebnisse legen nahe, dass dieser negative Effekt durch die vergleichsweise geringere Wertstiftung von Equity-Crowdfunding-Investoren verursacht wird. Diese geringere Wertstiftung lässt sich theoretisch durch verschiedene Defizite erklären: Erstens verfügen Equity-Crowdfunding-Investoren über weniger starke Kontrollmechanismen als traditionelle Risikokapitalgeber. Zweitens sind Equity-Crowdfunding-Investoren derzeit nicht in der Lage, ihr potenziell wertvolles Wissen und ihr großes Kontaktnetzwerk für die finanzierten Unternehmen zugänglich zu machen. Drittens verfügen Equity-Crowdfunding-Investoren über eine schlechtere Reputation als traditionelle Risikokapitalgeber.

Zur Beantwortung der zweiten Forschungsfrage stützen sich die Analysen des zweiten Aufsatzes auf einen einzigartigen Paneldatensatz zu Gründungsfinanzierung und Start-up-Entwicklung in Europa (genannt „VICO 4.0"). Zudem kommen erneut fortschrittliche empirische Methoden wie die zweistufige verallgemeinerte Momentenmethode (GMM-SYS), welche die inhärente Endogenität der VC-Finanzierung adressiert, zum Einsatz. Dieser Aufsatz trägt zur Erforschung von Selektions- und Wertstiftungseffekten von VC-Investoren bei, indem er Unterschiede zwischen VC-Investoren aufzeigt und somit ein differenzierteres Verständnis dieser Effekte schafft. Die Analysen zeigen, dass ein hoher Grad an Branchenspezialisierung der Wertstiftung von Investoren abträglich ist, was darauf hindeutet, dass vielfältige Erfahrung und nicht tiefes Branchenwissen die Grundlage für die erfolgreiche Portfolioarbeit von VC-Investoren bildet. Darüber hinaus zeigt die Analyse, dass eine hohe Kongruenz zwischen der Branchenspezialisierung des VC-Investors und den Eigenschaften eines Portfolio-Unternehmens zusätzlich schädigend auf die Wertstiftung wirkt. Aus theoretischer Sicht lässt sich dies durch eine höhere Wahrscheinlichkeit der Wissensaneignung durch den VC-Investor und die mögliche Informationsweitergabe an Wettbewerber des Portfoliounternehmens erklären. Nichtsdestotrotz deuten die Ergebnisse des zweiten Aufsatzes auch darauf hin, dass VC-Investoren unterschiedlich fähig darin sind, Unternehmen mit einem größeren inhärenten Wachstumspotenzial auszuwählen. Konkret zeigen die Ergebnisse, dass eine größere Branchenspezialisierung von VC-Investoren deren Fähigkeit, potenzialstarke Unternehmen innerhalb der jeweiligen Branche auszuwählen, positiv beeinflusst.

Der dritte Aufsatz stützt sich ebenfalls auf den Datensatz „VICO 4.0" und verwendet gleichfalls fortschrittliche Schätzverfahren einschließlich GMM-SYS und einer logistischen Regression für sehr seltene Ereignisse, um die dritte Forschungsfrage zu beantworten. Hierbei wird das Verhältnis zwischen denjenigen Investoren, die ein Syndikat anführen („Lead-Investoren") und ihren tatsächlichen bzw. potenziellen Co-Investoren vor dem Hintergrund der jeweils vorliegenden Branchenexpertise und den Anforderungen des Investitionsvorgangs untersucht. Der Aufsatz bietet eine gesamthafte Perspektive, die sowohl die Entscheidung von Lead-Investoren, ein Konsortium zu bilden als auch die Wahl ihrer Co-Investoren umfasst. Die Ergebnisse zeigen, dass VC-Investoren seltener ein Syndikat bilden, wenn sie über ein hohes Maß relevanter Branchenexpertise verfügen. Gleichermaßen ist es wahrscheinlicher, dass der Lead-Investor, welcher das Syndikat anführt, diejenigen potenziellen Co-Investoren für den Beitritt zu seinem Syndikat auswählt, die über eine höhere relevante Branchenexpertise im Bereich des jeweiligen Portfoliounternehmens verfügen. Dieser empirische Befund steht somit im Einklang mit theoretischen Argumenten, die besagen, dass spezialisiertes Branchenwissen eine kritische Ressource für VC-Investoren ist, da es Informationsasymmetrien reduziert und es VC-Investoren daher ermöglicht, bessere Anlageentscheidungen zu treffen. Darüber hinaus zeigen diese Ergebnisse, dass Investoren Syndikate auf opportunistische Weise bilden. Die Ergebnisse liefern zusätzliche Belege für die Ansicht, dass VC-Investoren dies tun, um Zugang zu komplementären Ressourcen zu erlangen.

Zusammengenommen leistet diese Dissertation mehrere theoretische Forschungsbeiträge zum Bereich der Risikokapitalfinanzierung sowie zu angrenzenden Forschungsgebieten. In erster Linie tragen die Aufsätze zum Forschungsstrang zu Investitionsauswahl und Wertstiftung von Risikokapitalgebern bei und ergänzen diesen in Breite und Tiefe. Der erste Aufsatz erweitert das wissenschaftliche Verständnis zur Wertstiftung von Risikokapitalgebern auf das Equity-Crowdfunding, welches ein zunehmend wichtiger Finanzierungsmechanismus für Start-ups ist, dessen Auswirkungen auf finanzierte Unternehmen bisher dennoch kaum erforscht waren. Darüber hinaus vertieft der zweite Aufsatz die wissenschaftlichen Erkenntnisse zur Investitionsauswahl und Wertstiftung von Investoren, indem er ein differenzierteres Verständnis der Heterogenität dieser Effekte schafft und aufzeigt, dass Investoren unterschiedlich fähig darin sind, potenzialstarke Unternehmen zu identifizieren und Mehrwert für diese Firmen zu stiften. Darüber hinaus bereichert diese Dissertation auch das Forschungsfeld der VC-Spezialisierung, indem sie den

Einfluss der Branchenspezialisierung auf die Ergebnisse in verschiedenen Phasen des Investitionsprozesses untersucht. Diese Phasen umfassen sowohl die Investitionsauswahl und -strukturierung als auch die anschließende Portfolioarbeit. Weiterhin ergänzt diese Dissertation den Forschungsstrang der VC-Syndizierung, indem sie eine gesamthafte Analyse von Syndikatsbildung und -komposition bietet. Darüber hinaus sind bestimmte Aspekte dieser Dissertation auch für weitere Forschungsrichtungen der Managementliteratur jenseits der Gründungsfinanzierung von Interesse. Beispielsweise tragen die Ergebnisse, die zeigen, wie VC-Investoren durch unterschiedliche Grade an Branchenspezialisierung relevante Fähigkeiten zur Auswahl und Weiterentwicklung von Portfoliofirmen erwerben, zur Erforschung des organisationalen Lernens bei. Zudem sind die Ergebnisse der Untersuchungen zu Equity-Crowdfunding auch für den Forschungsstrang zu „Open Strategy" relevant und wirken somit an einer Zusammenführung dieser Forschungsfelder mit. Im breiteren Kontext der Managementforschung ergänzen die Ergebnisse dieser Dissertation die sogenannte Ressourcentheorie, da sie spezifische Ressourcen identifizieren, die im Kontext der Gründungsfinanzierung wertvoll sind. Zudem stellt der Aufsatz über Equity-Crowdfunding auch die Agenturkostentheorie in den Kontext neuer digitaler Finanzierungsmodelle und bestätigt damit die fortdauernde Relevanz der Theorie im digitalen Zeitalter.

Des Weiteren halten die Ergebnisse dieser Forschungsarbeit auch eine Reihe praktischer Implikationen für verschiedene Akteure im Umfeld der Gründungsfinanzierung bereit. Erstens informiert diese Studie Regulierungsbehörden, Unternehmer und Betreiber von Equity-Crowdfunding-Plattformen über die aktuellen Defizite von Equity-Crowdfunding. Im derzeitigen Zustand ist Equity-Crowdfunding leider kein Allheilmittel für die strukturelle Knappheit von Risikokapital. Es bedarf vielmehr grundlegender Veränderungen durch Plattformbetreiber und Aufsichtsbehörden, um Equity-Crowdfunding als eine adäquate Finanzierungsalternative für Jungunternehmen zu etablieren. Darüber hinaus bietet diese Dissertation einen wichtigen, empirisch fundierten Einblick für VC-Investoren. Insbesondere die Ergebnisse des zweiten Aufsatzes deuten darauf hin, dass VC-Investoren mit einem Zielkonflikt hinsichtlich ihrer Branchenspezialisierung konfrontiert sind. Einerseits ist starke Branchenspezialisierung vorteilhaft, um potenzialstarke Unternehmen auszuwählen, andererseits ist ebendiese Branchenspezialisierung nachteilig für die Fähigkeit, Wertstiftung für Portfoliofirmen zu betreiben. Daher sollten VC-Fondsmanager auf ein optimales Maß an Branchenspezialisierung bzw. -diversifikation hinarbeiten, um ein Gleichgewicht zwischen Vorteilen für Investitionsauswahl und Wertstiftung zu finden, sodass die Fondsrenditen unter diesen Randbedingungen maximiert werden. Naturgemäß kann dieser Zielkonflikt zu Interessenkonflikten mit Unternehmern führen, deren Interesse es ist, von Wertstiftungsbeiträgen durch VC-Investoren zu profitieren. Somit sind diese Forschungsergebnisse auch für Unternehmer wertvoll. Darüber hinaus ermöglichen diese Ergebnisse spezifischere Interventionen von Regulierungsbehörden und politischen Entscheidungsträgern, da diese Akteure daran interessiert sein sollten, die Rahmenbedingungen so zu gestalten, dass die Wertstiftung durch VC-Investoren angeregt wird.

Zusammenfassend unterstreichen die Ergebnisse dieser Dissertation den bedeutenden und nachweisbaren Einfluss von Risikokapitalgebern auf die von ihnen finanzierten Unternehmen. Die vorliegende Arbeit fördert ein differenzierteres Verständnis der Selektions- und Wertstiftungseffekte im Bereich der Risikokapitalfinanzierung, insbesondere durch das Aufzeigen nuancierter Effekte innerhalb der Gruppe der VC-Investoren. Diese Erkenntnisse sollten daher auch bei zukünftigen Untersuchungen dieser Art Berücksichtigung finden.